T0287886

# NOMADIC PRESS

WWW.NOMADICPRESS.ORG

**MASTHEAD**
FOUNDING PUBLISHER
J. K. Fowler

ASSOCIATE EDITOR
Michaela S. Mullin

DESIGN
Jevohn Tyler Newsome

**MISSON STATEMENT** Through publications, events, and active community participation, Nomadic Press collectively weaves together platforms for intentionally marginalized voices to take their rightful place within the world of the written and spoken word. Through our limited means, we are simply attempting to help right the centuries' old violence and silencing that should never have occurred in the first place and build alliances and community partnerships with others who share a collective vision for a future far better than today.

**INVITATIONS** Nomadic Press wholeheartedly accepts invitations to read your work during our open reading period every year. To learn more or to extend an invitation, please visit: www.nomadicpress.org/invitations

**DISTRIBUTION**
Orders by teachers, libraries, trade bookstores, or wholesalers:

Nomadic Press Distribution
orders@nomadicpress.org
(510) 500-5162

Small Press Distribution
spd@spdbooks.org
(510) 524-1668 / (800) 869-7553

*Warriors for Justice: Our Future Has Its Eyes On You*

This book was made possible by a loving community of chosen family and friends, old and new.

For author questions or to book a reading at your bookstore, university/school, or alternative establishment, please send an email to info@nomadicpress.org.

Cover art: "Le Bien" by Isaac Vazquez Avila

Published by Nomadic Press, 111 Fairmount Avenue, Oakland, California 94611

First printing, 2022

Library of Congress Cataloging-in-Publication Data

Title: *Warriors for Justice: Our Future Has Its Eyes On You*
p. cm.
Summary: Rooted in a legacy of social movements for change, East Oakland youth and students from Urban Promise Academy in the Fruitvale district have created a social justice club known as Warriors for Justice. Over the last five years, they have compiled political speeches, news features and interviews, spoken word, poetry, street murals, and art that reflects their work as youth organizers and activists. Learn about what these young, inspiring leaders have to say about their journey, in *Warriors for Justice: Our Future Has Its Eyes on You*. They reflect on what it means to "be the change you want to see in the world," since "injustice anywhere is a threat to justice everywhere."

[1. YOUNG ADULT NONFICTION / Activism & Social Justice. 2. YOUNG ADULT NONFICTION / Science & Nature / Environmental Conservation & Protection. 3. POETRY / American / General. 4. ART / Graffiti & Street Art.] I. III. Title.

LIBRARY OF CONGRESS CONTROL NUMBER: 2021953490

ISBN: 978-1-955239-27-1

# WARRIORS FOR JUSTICE
## OUR FUTURE HAS ITS EYES ON YOU

### EDITED BY MICHAELA MULLIN

# WARRIORS FOR JUSTICE
## OUR FUTURE HAS ITS EYES ON YOU

EDITED BY MICHAELA MULLIN

**NOMADIC PRESS**

# CONTENTS

## POEMS

## RESOURCES

## READING GUIDE

# FOREWORD

What is the purpose of education in a time when crises are escalating and the future is so deeply uncertain? Every day, kids go to school and teachers work hard to teach them. But how do those hours in school prepare students for the actual future? How do students trust the teachings of adults when the system adults create is not only dehumanizing and kills members of their own communities, but is also careening towards an even more chaotic and dangerous future? What does it mean to a middle school student when science tells them that by the time they get to college, our world could well be locked into a spiraling disaster that will last for thousands of years?

I believe that Warriors for Justice (W4J) is a model of how young people, supported by teachers, can do meaningful work within this moment in history. W4J does not tell young people to first absorb passively, and then act at some distant time in the future. Rather, students learn by acting—taking real, meaningful, and significant action to change the world. Warriors for Justice offers a chance for the entire school and community to become part of the work for justice and survival.

As an educator for the past 20 years, and as a parent, I can't imagine a better gift to young people than the chance to be honest about our situation and to use their minds, hearts, and communities to fight for everything they love.

W4J is not a program that serves young people (though youth do seem to get a lot from being part of it). Rather, it is a way for young people to serve their communities, and to fight for their own value and promise. The group is not formed by theory or grant money, but by the caring and brilliance of the young people involved, and their adult supporter, the amazing Mx Cory.

The work W4J does is responsive and can be described as "emergent strategy." That is, when issues come up, it is a community that is ready to reflect and respond. This might look like how, when one 6th grade member uncovered some of the scary realities of climate change and reached out

to Mx. Cory about it, the group was poised to get involved in the work against the Dakota Access Pipeline. Because of the strength of the W4J community, they were able to go out into larger actions and workshops, and also come back to their "home base" at Urban Promise Academy (UPA), to reflect and support each other.

Another example occurred during one of the first times the Bay Area was blanketed in smoke in a really intense way. W4J was already meeting, in the hallway of the school, with sore throats and stinging eyes—to engage in analyses about why this was happening and who had access to mitigation measures, from air filters to N95 masks. Because the community was ready, W4J was able to collaborate *that day* to create and release a video declaring this a climate emergency.

W4J also provides an anchor and home for organizing their entire school community. When young people at UPA had the opportunity to be part of larger actions, there was an accessible, welcoming place for them to *stay involved*—something often missing in our movements. So, for example, if a student had a powerful experience speaking or drumming or painting at a climate strike, they had a place to go, the next week, to keep having (and analyzing) those experiences. And in turn, when some teachers threatened to stop students from attending strikes, there was an organized body at the school ready to push back with petitions and other forms of youth-generated pressure.

The reach of W4J is both deep and broad. It is deep, in that young people working with W4J grow and transform deeply—that is why many stay involved long after they leave middle school. But it is also broad, as W4J members have expressed their analysis and their vision nationally—from the Harvard School of Education to nationally published interviews and Op Eds, to speeches in front of government offices and in hearings, to conversations with parents, siblings, and others throughout the Fruitvale community.

The world would not be the same without Warriors for Justice, and I am so glad they are taking the time to document their work in this book.

**Carolyn Norr**
program director for Youth vs. Apocalypse

# INTRODUCTION

"We are the ones we've been waiting for."

**Hopi Elders**

Warriors for Justice is a social justice club that was started in 2015 by students at Urban Promise Academy, a middle school in the Fruitvale district of East Oakland. We met on Zoom to celebrate our five-year anniversary, in the midst of a global pandemic, to look back on the first five years together, and to think about our vision for the future. Two things came out of this anniversary celebration: members started our first chapter/branch at Envision Academy, and we decided to write this book as a way to tell our story. We realize it is important to grow, and as we grow, we will need to capture the story of our journey for future members. As artists of SF Jazz remind us, if we don't tell our story, who will?

It is urgent for young people to take action today. We are living in the middle of a global pandemic, in a world where we fear for our future due to catastrophic climate chaos and the impact of white supremacy, patriarchy, and capitalism. Through organizing, there is hope, strength, and power, and in the tradition of the Black Panther Party (originally called the Black Panther Party for Self-Defense), which started in our hometown, we believe in All Power to the People and want to Serve the People.

How do you build community power? We also want to share our story as a call to action, because it is possible to find like-minded people who can work together to build a club or organization as a means to address political issues and the needs of the community. All you need to get started is to find two other people and form a core group! (It helps to have at least two people in each grade.) Other than that, it takes passion, commitment to see things through, and consistent nurturing, as for a plant, to keep things alive and moving.

We organize based on a framework of mass-line organizing, in the tradition of the Chinese and Filipino movements, to arouse (educate, raise consciousness), organize (build organizations), and mobilize (take political action). This includes conducting social investigations to identify the felt needs of the community, along with community resources.

As we approach our six-year anniversary, our oldest founding members are in their second year of college. Our membership started with committees, to work on a program co-sponsored by Af3IRM SF Bay Area (the Association of Feminists Fighting Fascism, Imperialism, Refeudalization, and Marginalization), a transnational feminist, anti-imperialist, women of color organization, as part of Amnesty International's 16 Days of Activism to End Gender-Based Violence. In terms of race, ethnicity, and cultural background, our first members were Guatemalan (indigenous Mam-speakers), Yemeni, Black / African American, Filipino American, and Chinese American. In terms of gender identity, all students at that time identified as young women or girls. Our school is located blocks away from International Boulevard, and one of the campaigns and political issues that brought us together included Af3IRM's Purple Rose campaign to end the sex trafficking of women and children, with an event at EastSide Arts Alliance and workshops at Cal's Empowering Women of Color Conference. At a time when the Black Lives Matter movement and the Say Her Name campaign were in its early years, our first chant-leading opportunities came when members participated in Oakland's Reclaim MLK's Radical Legacy March, with the Anti-Police Terror Project and Abundant Beginnings. With coaching from Guisela Ramos, our members participated in the OUSD Martin Luther King, Jr. Oratorical Festival. Public speaking that year also included a panelist on community violence at the African American Policy Forum's Breaking the Silence Town Hall for Women and Girls of Color. In this first year, we also helped a member and her family find peace, by mobilizing the community for information about her older brother's murder, which was becoming a cold case. In our second year, we built relationships with Sogorea Te' Land Trust organizers, as the Ohlone people work to protect sacred sites and burial grounds, including the shellmounds of Emeryville and Berkeley.

A turning point came in 2016, our second year, when Angelika Soriano, then a sixth-grader, became very scared about the future of our planet. At this time, indigenous organizers were actively resisting the development of the Dakota Access Pipeline, with the call to "Kill the Black Snake" and #NoDAPL. We were invited to attend a conference at MetWest High School, where we attended a workshop on the campaign and the call to divest from Wells Fargo, an investor in this pipeline project. The workshop was organized by Families Against Fossil Fuels, and facilitated by Whitney Dwyer and Carolyn Norr. Carolyn invited us to attend an upcoming climate justice workshop, and since Angelika had worked on animation about lead poisoning and environmental justice for her science class, we decided to host a workshop on art, activism, and animation. There, we learned about the No Coal in Oakland campaign.

Taking political action locally against developer Phil Tagami, through the No Coal in Oakland campaign, was a pivotal moment in the story of Warriors for Justice. Through this campaign, the founding members of Youth vs. Apocalypse met and worked together for the first time, including Carolyn Norr, Isha Clarke, and Angelika Soriano. Other members, like Tanaya Patton, Sonia Mendoza Pablo, and Sophia Lopez Garcia note that attendance at these actions were significant in their political growth. We received national press coverage, through outlets like Ms. Magazine and Sierra Club Magazine, which featured Angelika Soriano as one of the youth campaign spokespersons. In addition, this climate justice organizing influenced the instruction at Urban Promise Academy, where 6th-grade featured an interdisciplinary, project-based unit on environmental racism for the end-of-the-year Expo (like Open House). Also provided were grade-level field trips to support students who spoke at press conferences on the steps of San Francisco City Hall and testified to the Environmental Protection Agency on the Clean Power Plan.

This led to the development of Youth vs. Apocalypse, "a diverse group of young climate justice activists based in the Bay Area, who are working together to lift the voices of youth, in particular, youth of color, and to fight for a livable climate and an equitable, sustainable, and just world," with Warriors for Justice as some of the youngest founding members and campaign spokespeople.

We met César Cruz in the fall of 2018, as part of the 6th-grade

Humanities unit on the school slogan, "Developing Scholars, Warriors, and Artists." César received his doctorate from the Harvard Graduate School of Education, and he encouraged Warriors for Justice to look into a conference known as the Alumni of Color Conference. He said that people would be interested in hearing about a youth-led, school-based, intersectional, social justice club at the middle school level in the Fruitvale district of East Oakland. After applying to host a workshop, Warriors for Justice, through the support of César, family, and community, were able to fundraise to bring five youth and two adults to the conference. After months of preparation, just as members were ready to leave, the Oakland Education Association Teachers' Strike started. With some core members still in Oakland, Warriors for Justice members, like Adam Al-Shugaa, were able to maintain an active presence on the picket line.

Within days of leaving for the Harvard conference, members were part of a youth contingent, along with members of Bay Area Earth Guardians and Youth vs. Apocalypse, that confronted Senator Dianne Feinstein, urging her to support the Green New Deal. This exchange went viral and led to a march of an estimated 2,000 people in response to her refusal to listen to the youth.

For many Warriors for Justice members, this was their first experience flying on an airplane, leaving the state of California, or seeing snow. The trip would not have been possible without the support of Ashley Herring and her family, Mama Linda, and the work of blackyard arts, "centering RADICAL self transformation and BLACK youth," who shared their home and connected us with neighbors, provided us with shelter, nourishment, a liberatory space, and love. We visited Wah Lum Kung Fu in Malden, spoke at Steve Seidel's graduate school of education art class, went on a walking tour of Harvard University, and visited local museums. We came back with a strong core group of members who identified themselves as youth activists. In the fall of 2019, this team was ready to take on leadership roles in the Global Climate Strike, organized with Youth vs. Apocalypse, resulting in an estimated 10,000 people in San Francisco, as part of a global action in 4,500 locations, 150 countries, and on all 7 continents.

Over the years, our members have experienced powerful, personal transformations. Based on the slogan from Urban Promise Academy, our members embody the idea of what it means to be "Developing Artists, Scholars, and Warriors." The following pages represent a collection of poems, narratives, speeches, op-eds, photos, murals, art, and interviews, to capture some of these moments.

In March of 2019, climate scientists and the United Nations said we have 11 years (to around 2030) before our planet reaches a tipping point. If you take the amount of time Warriors for Justice has existed and multiply this times two, that is the total amount of time we are talking about. Our oldest founding members will be 28-years-old by then. While this seems like a long time from now, time passes in the blink of an eye. That's why what Malcolm X said makes sense: "The future belongs to those who prepare for it today," and why we believe that our future has its eyes on us. Will you be on the right side of hxstory (the x is on purpose—to be gender inclusive and as a shout-out to Malcolm X) and be a Warrior for Justice with us?

**Cory Jong and Christopher Soriano**

# WARRIORS FOR JUSTICE
## ORGANIZATIONAL INFORMATION

# WARRIORS FOR JUSTICE LOGO (2015)

Heidy Chales Mendoza, Iyyah Zareef-Mustafa
& Agustin "Base" Barajas

"Warriors for Justice Logo" (2015), designed by Heidy Chales
Mendoza, Iyyah Zareef-Mustafa & Agustin "Base" Barajas

# MISSION STATEMENT

WARRIORS FOR JUSTICE WAS FORMED IN 2015, BY MIDDLE SCHOOL-AGED YOUTH FROM URBAN PROMISE ACADEMY IN THE FRUITVALE DISTRICT OF EAST OAKLAND.

OUR MISSION IS TO COME TOGETHER TO FIGHT FOR OUR RIGHTS, BUILD LEADERSHIP SKILLS, MAKE A DIFFERENCE IN OUR COMMUNITY, ADDRESS THE ISSUES THAT ARE HAPPENING IN OUR WORLD, AND LET OUR VOICES BE HEARD.

# MEMBERSHIP AGREEMENT

## Recruitment process

**1** Group should approve new members

**2** If someone is interested in joining, but cannot attend community events, they should attend meetings consistently

**3** For new members: attend at least 2-3 community events to meet members

# MEMBERSHIP AGREEMENT
## (continued)

## Membership Agreements

**1. Follow** Community Agreements and school rules

**2. State your needs** use restorative justice **to deal with conflicts**

**3.** Be a **role model** and a **leader**

**4. Develop as a scholar, warrior, and artist**

**5.** Think about how we represent W4J **be an upstander**

**6. Stay on track** with your academics

**7. Check in with each other**

**8.** Be **open-minded, respectful, inclusive,** and **patient**

**9.** Attend meetings and events consistently and **communicate** when you are not available

**10.** Work as a **team** and **collaborate**

**11.** Stay focused and listen attentively during meetings **(one mic, process check)**

**Have fun!**

# FOUNDING EVENT FLYER: 16 DAYS OF ACTIVISM AGAINST GENDER-BASED VIOLENCE

**16 Days of Activism Against Gender-Based Violence**

2015 Theme: "From Peace in the Home to Peace in the World: Make Education Safe for All!"

*Organized by "UPA Warriors for Justice," 6th and 7th grade Urban Promise Academy students*
*Co-sponsored by the UPA Family Resource Center*
*& AF3IRM, a Transnational Feminist Woman of Color organization.*

**Friday 12/4/15**
4:00-5:00 pm
**Art Room**
(next to the gym and parking lot)
**Urban Promise Academy (UPA)**
3031 East 18th St.
Oakland, CA 94601
Light refreshments provided
FREE DRESS PASS FOR UPA STUDENTS

Topics to include:
#SayHerName, Black Lives Matter, and police brutality as it impacts their lives as African American young women; the war in Yemen, Islamophobia, and access to education, as it impacts their lives as Muslim young women; the current case of US military rape/murder of a transgender woman near Subic Bay in the Philippines, brought up by Filipino young women; violence in Guatemala.

# FIRST YEAR (2015–2016)

UPA Warriors for Justice

Urban Promise Academy Warriors for Justice chant leading on the bullhorn at #ReclaimMLKDay 2016

16 Days of Activism to End Gender Based Violence

OUSD MLK Oratorical Contest: "Still I Rise"

AF3IRM Purple Rose Dialogue on Sex Trafficking at EastSide Arts & Empowering Women of Color Conference at UC Berkeley

Poster–making for Immigrant Rights
"Protection Not Detention!"

Breaking the Silence
Town Hall Meeting for Women and Girls of Color

# WARRIORS FOR JUSTICE FLAG

**"Warriors for Justice flag" design adapted by The Grease Diner**

# COMMUNITY GARDEN PROJECT
July 2020 – February 2021

Before (July 15th)

Stage One Done! Cleared
2 planter boxes, 3 benches
& 2 concrete planters

After (July 29th)

9

# 5-YEAR ANNIVERSARY PAINTING

Iyyah Zareef-Mustafal

"To me, W4J is unity and a safe place for student voices to be heard. W4J was created to address discriminatory experiences with classmates, attend events, create protests, and join the fight for change. We address problems such as sex trafficking, police brutality, and more. This painting represents the vision of W4J along with the opportunities that organizing creates. W4J is influence and strength, born in Oakland."

**Iyyah Zareef-Mustafal**

# WARRIORS FOR JUSTICE
## SOLIDARITY STATEMENTS

# Youth vs. Apocalypse
## Isha Clarke

It was young people from Warriors for Justice that brought me into The Movement. In 2017, we stood together, facing Phil Tagami, a powerful man who was trying to poison our community and further destroy our planet's climate. I watched my W4J peers confront this power-holder with undeniable truth and a passion that deeply moved me. Without these young people, I would not be who I am today. Warriors for Justice is an incredible organization that is held up by young people who will change the world. I am still moved by the work, dedication, and brilliance of these youth. All my love and respect to W4J!

# Blackyard Arts
## Ashley Herring

The time I spent with the Warriors for Justice and Cory changed my life when they visited Cambridge, MA, for their conference at Harvard University. I was able to listen and learn from the realistic and most authentic youth organizing. Cory facilitated a space that allowed for the youth to ACTUALLY lead!!! What I witnessed were young people who had very deep ideas and thoughts about how to take action, and it was rooted in values and community. It was a blessing to have that experience, and they should be lifted and honored for their organizing. I'm a further transformed older person because these young folks shared their knowledge and space with me. One of those moments, I KNEW the world I lived in would be shaped and lifted up because of them.

# Earth Guardians Bay Area Crew

BoomShake Music has been so proud and inspired to drum with the youth leaders of Warriors for Justice over the past few years. We are always impressed by W4J members' deep commitment to justice, knowledge of movement-building and social issues, creative ideas, excellent chanting skills, and great drum beats! Together, we have played for youth climate strikes and May Day immigrants' rights actions. We are excited to be back in the streets together soon and to see all the change that W4J members make in the world.

# Af3IRM SF Bay Area

Congratulations, Warriors for Justice, for five years of radical action, education, and community activism! The SF Bay Area chapter of AF3IRM has had the privilege of working with W4J over the last few years. From co-presenting at UPA on the topic of gender-based violence, to participating in the Sunrise Ceremony in Alcatraz in solidarity with Indigenous communities, to most recently, highlighting their inspiring work at our first ever School of Women's Activism. We are so grateful for these opportunities for intergenerational activism. We know that our youth are the future. And together, we will continue building the path towards liberation.

# Agency by Design, Oakland
## Paula Mitchell & Brooke Toczylowski, Co-Directors

Dear Warriors for Justice Team,

Congratulations on reaching your five year anniversary!

Your growth over these past several years has been inspiring to witness. Mural projects, social actions, intergenerational work, bringing in your younger brothers and sisters, and having students continue their activism once leaving Urban Promise Academy, shows the power of your group. Continuing to move forward with your projects amidst the global pandemic shows your dedication to making change. You are creating a legacy of activism and caring whose impact will be felt for years to come.

You exemplify what we hope for all youth- the ability to be critical, empathetic thinkers, with the ability to use your voice and talents to change the systems in which we live for the better.

We are honored to be able to support the work you have been doing to help transform your community and the wider world to become a more just place.

We wish you another 5 years of making good trouble and doing good work!

In Community,

The Agency by Design Oakland Leadership Team
Paula Mitchell & Brooke Toczylowski Co-Directors

# Oakland in the Middle
## Geoff Vu

Congrats on 5 years!

Congratulations to the UPA Warriors for Justice! You stand among a great lineage of local and global activists who push us to think critically, engage with our neighbors, and speak truth to power — and not only when it's easy. As a collective, you have demonstrated that you are powerful beyond measure, and as individuals, you never shy away from standing on your own two feet, rooted in your own convictions, and strengthened seemingly from an intrinsic belief that you are never alone. This is probably one of the most profound features of your young but wise organization. You will not be divided and you will not be silenced.

Here's to many many more!

Siempre adelante!

# Urban Promise Academy
## Tierre Mesa, Principal

Warriors for Justice has grown over time to become a critical student leadership group within our school community. Their work to advocate for the issues that matter to them, and to organize other students to do the same, builds each student's self-confidence, tapping into their innate leadership capabilities, and empowers them to be change-makers within their community. W4J also continually reminds adults of the power of listening to the voices and needs of our students and to be in solidarity with our students, instead of centering education on what adults feel that students need.

# Gender Sexuality Alliance - Rainbow Club
## Crystal Barajas Barr

Over the years, the UPA GSA-Rainbow Club and Warriors for Justice have shared several members, demonstrating that social justice work is indeed intersectional! Many times, W4J has shown true solidarity with the LGBTQ+ community, by creating posters and standing up for Queer and Trans rights by challenging homophobic mentalities in and out of school. We have been proud to work with W4J, whether it's on a collaborative community mural, attending actions, or by listening and asking how we can be a part of the meaningful work they are doing with our communities. We stand with W4J, and know that deep, sustainable social change can only happen by building relationships across communities, which requires trust and solidarity with our struggles. Thank you, W4J, and congratulations on over 5 years of youth-led radical, anti-patriarchal, and inclusive organizing!

# UPA Music Club
## Gretchen Baglyos

Collaborating with the Warriors for Justice has inspired our UPA Music Students to raise their voices in activism! Music is at the heart of social justice movements, and working in solidarity with the W4J has allowed us to join in youth-led protests and marches as drummers, chant leaders, and singers. Together, with our partners at BoomShake music, UPA music students and W4J students were part of the drum core in the 2019 Oakland May Day March for Immigrant and Workers' Rights. The next fall, we added even more students to our drum core, and created original chants to march in the 2019 Youth-Led Climate Strike in San Francisco. Taking part in these and other demonstrations with Warriors for Justice asks us to step up as scholars, warriors, and artists, as we fight for our rights with the power of music. It has been an honor to collaborate with the W4J, and we look forward to more partnerships in 2022!

# WARRIORS FOR JUSTICE
## POEMS

# LOLO
## Angelika Soriano

Hello, my name is Angelika, and I will be telling a poem about my grandpa, Floro, or in my language, Tagalog, Lolo Floro. My lolo died 4 years ago, and I thought I would represent him in the Day of the Dead. Also I want to thank Ms. Guisela for helping me make this poem. I hope you enjoy it.

My family and I are having a family reunion.
*My uncles, aunts, cousins, and my lolo—my **whole** family is here.*
Kids are in separate teams, we're playing egg on a spoon.
I see both teams ready to go, but I'm nervous because I'm thinking I am going to lose.
I look around before I go, and then,
*I saw my lolo smiling.*
It made me confident instead of fearful, and then I heard a person on a mic say it
    was going to start,
and a loud beep went off. I woke up next to my rainy window sill.
The rain was pounding through my window like it was breaking in.
I saw my alarm clock next to my ear while turning it off. Then I shivered like a soul
    was going through me.
Then I remembered my lolo in my dream: the last thing I remember was
*him smiling,*
how helpful he was in my life.
I remember seeing him for the first time and I can see how hard he worked for his family,
how kind he was to people, and that they depended on him.
I remember he told me and my sister stories about a man named Jesus who helped
    us beings and our world.
My lolo said that he will be seeing him.
I remember he was the one who made us laugh the most and would never get mad

at us no matter how bad it was.
Like when me, my sister, and cousin locked him out of our apartment.
I remember he told me how he sacrificed his life to feed his family, instead of
getting an education.
He would grow rice for his family
no matter how hot the scorching sun was.

I can see him,

> Still smiling
> Still working
> Still sacrificing for his family.

I remember the last place we met was in a hospital, and talked, laughed, and had
a blast. But one day the hospital called and said,
He's gone, he died because of high blood pressure.
I froze and felt the tears coming down, out of control.
I visited him, covered in white sheets.
I remember I went to his funeral in the Philippines and everyone cried.

I saw my lolo in his casket, laying there like a doll.
I remember not knowing anyone but feeling sad.
My last words to him were, I love you so much and I hope we can see each other
again.

> I can see him,
> Still smiling
> Still working
> Still in my dreams.

# WE ARE THE PEOPLE

## Angelika Soriano, Tanaya Patton, Mariah Lazalde
*(originally performed at the 38ᵗʰ Annual OUSD
MLK Oratorical Festival)*

Our president says women are objects.
We need to be treated as humans.
You will not treat us like puppets.
You won't put strings on us.
We are not fragile.
We are strong.

We will stand.

You say I don't have a voice because I'm a kid.
I'm not voiceless.
I will speak!
I will raise my fist up!
We are the children!
We are the next generation.

We are strong.

We stand with black people
Who face racism and discrimination because of their color.
Who get killed by police, thinking they are armed.
Whose lives matter.
BLACK LIVES MATTER!

We are the people!

We stand with indigenous people.
People native to this land
Who teach us to care for mother earth.
NO to the North Dakota access pipeline!
NO to contaminating our water with oil!
I stand with Standing Rock!

We raise our fist high!

We stand with the LGBTQ community.
The right to feel safe.
To be who you are meant to be.
You are human.

We will stand.
We are strong.
We are the people.

My family has taught me to be a leader.
So I stand with all people who bleed.
Don't be afraid to speak up.
Raise your fist up.

# PROTECT THE WEST BERKELEY SHELLMOUND

## Angelika Soriano, Sonia Mendoza Pablo

Public Comment for Berkeley City Council Meeting

We are here today to say
Shellmound site should not increase profits,
They should honor Indigenous People's Rights.

When you find resting bodies in sacred land,
In the past you dug their graves and sent their remains to UC Berkeley.
Today, when Indigenous people demand to be part of the process, you never call back.
Why do people destroy history?
Why bother touching sacred land that is not yours.
Would you rather have a parking lot built over you or rather rest in peace.

We are here today to say
Shellmound site should not increase profits,
They should honor Indigenous People's Rights.

Why are people like this?
Turning human existence and humanity into insanity.
The people that built Grocery Outlet (Bargain Market) on 5700 years of sacred land should be ashamed of themselves.
How would it feel if we built a parking lot on your graveyard?
Why should we even shop there, if we don't know the secrets buried under this mall?
Respect Indigenous People's LAND.

# OUSD MLK ORATORICAL FESTIVAL SPEECH
## Santiago Preciado-Cruz

Inspired by Civil Rights Activist Dr. Martin Luther King Jr. and German Pastor Martin Knee-mola

Injustice anywhere affects the balance of everybody and everything; let me explain.

They came for the Palestinians, stole their land, occupied and bombed their people, but it doesn't even make it to our History books, and most people do nothing because they are not Palestinian.

Then they go after women, where women work double the amount of men and receive half the pay, where women have to start #MeToo movements just to stop the harassment, and most do nothing because they are not women.

Then they go after immigrants, where families are separated and children are thrown in cages, and most do nothing because they are not immigrants.

Then they go after People of Color, where peaceful protestors are tear gassed, and people are invaded in their homes and killed wrongfully, and it seems that the only time they matter is after they have been murdered, and someone builds a # movement. And most do nothing because they aren't People of Color.

Then they go after Indigenous people, where hair is chopped off, land is stolen, and people are rounded up in reservations, and most do nothing, because they are not Indigenous people.

Then they go after the disabled, where they are constantly left out of opportunities and are disregarded, dishonored and disrespected, and most do nothing because they aren't disabled.

Then they go after the Muslims, where people who are just living their religion are attacked and called terrorists, and most do nothing, because they are not Muslim.

Then they go after LGBTQ+ people, where people are hated and are oppressed for who they are, and most do nothing, because they aren't LGBTQ+.

Then they go after you, and no one is left to help you.

If we keep up this vicious cycle of being bystanders, everyone will be hurt and nothing good will come from it. This is why the late Dr. King warned us that injustice anywhere threatens justice everywhere. That's why the late John Lewis asked us to get into "Good Trouble." Stand with Palestinians as we **reclaim** the land, Stand with Females and demand **more** than just equal pay and an end to harassment. Stand with Immigrants and demand full citizenship because **no** human being is illegal. Stand with People of Color as we **end** white supremacy **and** demand true justice for all. Stand with Indigenous people as we **demand** reparations. Standing with the Disabled may mean more than **sitting** in their shoes. It means we listen, and we stand up in solidarity. Stand with Muslims as we **end** travel bans and Islamophobia. Stand with LGBTQ+ people as we end homophobia, transphobia, and let's normalize being who you are. That's how **we** restore balance, stand up for each other, and exemplify solidarity for **all**.

**Thank you,**
**Santiago PC**

# UNTITLED
## Angelica Perkins

*(from Warriors for Justice Founding Event, December 4, 2015: 16-Days of Activism Against Gender-Based Violence, "From Peace in the Home to Peace in the World: Make Education Safe for All!")*

We are broken down and beaten up
We are strength in the flesh
We are uneducated, unenlightened, and just plain unenjoyable
We are that one fully-bloomed flower in a meadow of grass
We are jailbirds, crooks, and unworthy
We are hardworking, underestimated, underpaid
We are stereotyped and put in a category
And we are taken advantage of
We are food stamps, welfare, and poverty
We are strength in the numbers
We are the next generation and we dare to care

Not to be racist but
Nigga is used by the light or dark skinned male or female
To suppress the memory of the white man whipping at our souls
Because I'm saying nigga, not nigger
So of course there's a huge difference
Because by us saying it amongst ourselves it is given to us by choice
Because nigga isn't that bad
It's what I am, right?
It's what this dark skin makes me
It's what these hood ebonics make me
It's what Oakland makes me
Proof - if I'm applying for a job
and I check the "I am Black" box

They give it to the White girl
Even though I have way more experience than she does
Proof - the average Black little girl would rather have
The White "good" doll than the Black "bad" doll
Proof - there's a predominantly White city right in the middle of Oakland
Because "eh - we don't want that nigga"
Used to describe my skin as dirty, not beautiful bronze
Nigga, the name of a secret club that invites only the people with that unholy skin in
That word that we use mostly around our friends
That word that disappoints our ancestors
Nigga, weakness turned into a strength
That word meant to make us feel like nothing
Meant to tear our insides out
That word meant to be used as an anchor
While we are the boats and the White man is the ocean pulling us in any direction
he pleases
Now used by Blacks, Asians, Latinas, Native Americans and Whites,
Because it slips
Because we've made it okay
Nigga, the chain between the boat and the anchor
Used to describe my skin as dirty not beautiful blond

# AMERICA

## Kai Hong

America.
The country that stands for freedom.
The country that represents freedom.
Where is our freedom?
There is police brutality,
Racism,
People hated for their religion,
Discrimination.
We will not be free until the color of our skin does not matter.
We will not be free until police actually try to protect us from hurting.
We will not be free until we are seen as equals,
Until we are seen as people.
We will not be free until we are together.

# I BELIEVE
## Christopher Soriano

I believe that people shouldn't have to fear their lives and rights being taken
away from them
I believe that we and I have the right to fresh air and water
I believe that I should feel like I belong in society no matter what race, culture,
color of skin I am
I believe that People of Color should feel accepted and safe
However, our system was built on the roots of hate, such as oppression
Such as capitalism
Such as white supremacy
Such as colonialism
Such as systemic racism and more
I believe that we should abolish and dismantle these unsustainable, inequitable
systems that deem People of Color as disposable
I believe that humanity's worst enemy is... ourselves

# WON'T YOU CELEBRATE WITH ME

## Santiago Preciado-Cruz

Won't you celebrate with me, that every day I have breathed the sweet air of our amazing earth, that every day I have eaten the good foods of our lush planet. Won't you celebrate with me that I have the sight to see the beauty and the goodness of the earth. That I have the ability to get out of bed and walk around, RUN around, in the grass, the trees, the streets that we have created. Come celebrate the life that we have the privilege to live.

# WARRIORS FOR JUSTICE
## NARRATIVES

# STUDENT NARRATIVE
## Kai Hong

I met W4J members first at a climate march—I forget which one exactly—but remember that it was an amazing and fun experience. We were all chanting and shouting and it gave me an amazing feeling...like I was actually doing something for once, like I was actually helping with something big. It felt like there had been something inside me that only came out in times like that, like that thing wanted to do more, I wanted to do more. We walked and walked, yelling at the people bringing our world down. It amazed me, the amount of people that actually wanted to change the world for the better, the amount of people who cared about their planet. It was also the first time I learned about how much power I, as a youth, have. I could do something, I could change the world, and I wasn't about to throw something like that away.

A few weeks later, at my school, Urban Promise Academy, or UPA for short, I'm standing outside the door that, little to my knowledge, would change my life. It was right after my last class for the day; I had been sent by my sixth grade humanities teacher, Ms.Lisa, who, when I asked her about joining the Warriors for Justice, pointed me right to that door. I could hear my heart beating with the force of a grizzly bear threatening to rip right out of my chest, but I walked in, scared about what awaited me. The teacher of the classroom (and the adult leader of Warriors for Justice) told me I could do my homework at one of the tables in the front of the room, but I had already done half of it, so I finished that up. I saw some people (all at least a grade above me) sitting around some tables pushed together to form a big square. One of the seventh graders invited me over, so I sat down awkwardly at one of the seats facing the front of the room, feeling like a weirdo thinking about what was going to happen to me and if I would make a good first impression. Once the table started to fill up a bit more we all introduced ourselves. I was surprised at how there were pretty much no other sixth graders there. They started their meeting and it felt foreign; I had no idea what they were talking about. Everyone seemed so smart, like they really were ready to change the world right then and there. But me... me? I was struggling to understand what they were talking about, much less actually contribute to the conversation. I felt like a dumb little fir tree in a HUGE forest of redwoods. I learned some amazing things but I was still not feeling like I could be a part of the group. I was really intimidated by everyone and I still didn't know if I wanted to join.

I talked to my parents about it, and to myself, but I was scared I would take more away from the club than give to it. I kept thinking about what would happen if I joined. After a lot of thinking, I decided to join and am really glad I did, because since then, I have made tons of new friends and learned so much from the Warriors for Justice about social justice and the brokenness of the planet we call home; I am happy to be playing my part in making it a better place.

# WARRIORS FOR JUSTICE
## INTERVIEWS*

*All articles are reprinted as originally published.

ENVIRONMENT

## A 12-Year-Old Warrior for Justice

11/13/2017 by ANTONIA JUHASZ

Angelika Soriano suffered her first asthma attack in the fourth grade, though she didn't realize what it was at the time. She was walking to school in her Fruitvale neighborhood of East Oakland, California when pain gripped her body. She began to wheeze and cough. Unable to get sufficient air into her lungs, she found herself weakening until she was too tired to continue forward.

As luck would have it, her sister, Angeline, just two years her senior, also suffers from the disease. After getting a ride home, Angelika's diagnosis was easy to derive—as she quickly regained her breath using her sister's inhaler.

Photo by Antonia Juhasz

The children of Filipino immigrants, Angelika and Angeline are not alone. In East Oakland, where 93 percent of residents are people of color, children are more than twice as likely to visit an emergency room or be hospitalized for asthma than those in the county of Alameda overall, according to the Alameda County Public Health Department. A leading culprit identified by the Department is the disproportionally high amount of outdoor air pollution where they live—among the highest pollution rates in the state—caused by an over-concentration of motor vehicles, refineries and power plants.

# "A 12-YEAR-OLD WARRIOR FOR JUSTICE"

## Angelika Soriano, interviewed by Antonia Juhasz for *Ms. Magazine* (11/13/2017)

Angelika Soriano suffered her first asthma attack in the fourth grade, though she didn't realize what it was at the time. She was walking to school in her Fruitvale neighborhood of East Oakland, California when pain gripped her body. She began to wheeze and cough. Unable to get sufficient air into her lungs, she found herself weakening until she was too tired to continue forward.

As luck would have it, her sister, Angeline, just two years her senior, also suffers from the disease. After getting a ride home, Angelika's diagnosis was easy to derive—as she quickly regained her breath using her sister's inhaler. The children of Filipino immigrants, Angelika and Angeline are not

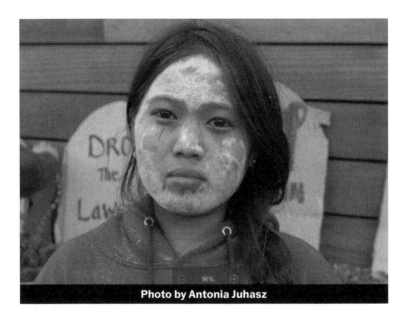

**Photo by Antonia Juhasz**

alone. In East Oakland, where 93 percent of residents are people of color, children are more than twice as likely to visit an emergency room or be hospitalized for asthma than those in the county of Alameda overall, according to the Alameda County Public Health Department. A leading culprit identified by the Department is the disproportionally high amount of outdoor air pollution where they live—among the highest pollution rates in the state—caused by an over-concentration of motor vehicles, refineries and power plants.

A little more than two and half years later, Angelika, now a remarkably mature and composed 12-year-old, organizes to protect not only the quality of the air she breathes, but on behalf of everyone's environment and climate. I meet Angelika as she recounts some of this story to a group of about 100 fellow middle- and high-school students, predominantly youth of color from low-income East and West Oakland. They are joined by teachers and parents, all gathered together on Halloween eve. Like Angelika, many are costumed in zombie face paint, having just finished marching through the affluent and exclusive Oakland Hills neighborhood. They did not come to ask for candy. Rather they have led a "Zombie March on Coal" from a local park to the private home of local developer Phil Tagami. Carrying banners and signs reading, "Oakland vs. Coal" and "Stop the Tagami Coal-Pacolypse" they are here to protest Tagami's plans to build a coal export terminal in West Oakland. If approved, it would be the largest such terminal on the West Coast, taking in train shipments of coal from Utah, with plans to potentially export millions of tons of coal annually. Tagami's plan fits nicely with the Trump administration's repeal of the Clean Power Plan and frequent pledges to increase U.S. coal production and "end the war on coal."

Tagami's house is festooned with ghouls of its own. A tall green Frankenstein mannequin and a grey bloodied skeleton dressed in rags stand guard on opposite ends of his sprawling second-story balcony, arms outstretched and looming over the protesting children gathered on the street below. The first floor of the home is well hidden behind a low grey-green raised cement wall, behind which stands a much taller red wood fence. All of which tower above Angelika as she walks to the front of the crowd, her back to Tagami's house, and takes the microphone attached to a small speaker placed in a baby stroller. Behind her, the youth have propped grey cardboard tombstones along Tagami's fence that read, "RIP Health," "RIP Lungs" and "RIP Clean Air."

Angelika is easy to overlook at first. Her voice is small, as is her body, which all but disappears inside an oversized thick green cotton sweatshirt hanging to her knees, with the name of her middle school, Urban Promise Academy, stitched in gold on the right-hand side. Her hair is tied in a thick black braid that ropes around her neck and hangs down her chest. I never see a smile cross her face, which is etched in white and red zombie paint. "I know I might be little," Angelika begins. "But I make a huge impact on this earth."

With these words, all attention turns, unwavering, to Angelika. She recites a spoken-word poem she has written, which she now addresses personally to Tagami. At first, she later recounts, she was frightened. But then, looking at those around her, "I saw that they are one of me," she explained. "I became very brave and courageous."

"Coal," she begins, pausing for effect.

"The beast that once lived under the ground has risen.

Coal.

The dirty beast. The dirty dusty rock that is invisible but visible to smell.

Coal.

The laughing beast. The beast who would be glad to hear the screams of people saying, "I can't breathe!" and fall to their knees trying to stay conscious before they became nothing.

Coal."

Angelika is a Warrior for Justice. It is the name of a club at her school founded and led by her teacher, Cory Jong. Jong stands serene as she listens intently to Angelika, little emotion visible across her zombie-white painted face, her eyes and lips blackened, and a white N95 protective facemask resting on her head. A Chinese-American, Jong is a member of AF3IRM, "a national organization of women engaged in transnational feminist, anti-imperialist activism and dedicated to the fight against oppression in all its forms," according to its website. They organize under the slogan, "a woman's place is at the head of the struggle."

At age 40, Jong is in her 12th year of teaching. She founded Warriors for Justice a little over two years ago. Until this year, all of its members were girls, ages 11 to 14. Jong wanted to engage her students in advocacy and social justice on the issues that most directly impact them in their community, she tells me. The students pick the topics—which have included sex trafficking, violence, environmental racism and climate change. She has found great support both at the school and among parents. Warriors for Justice joins other clubs espousing feminist principles, including Girls Inc. of Alameda., that have worked to empower the girls to not just participate in today's action, but to lead it.

Brooke Anderson of Climate Workers, a membership organization of rank-and-file union and nonunion workers advocating for climate justice in the Bay Area, also helped with the organizing. "You can tell the youth were in the lead," she says. "This is way more fun than anything that we would have done!"

Angelika says that many of the other girls at her school are shy and sometimes afraid to speak out. She is proud that she can do so on their behalf. She chooses this particular issue because, "the coal dust could go anywhere: the water, the air, into everyone's bodies, and it could affect rates of asthma—more people having asthma. It can harm the environment overall and the climate."

Angelika first learned about climate change when she was in elementary school. Her older sister then introduced her to the idea that "maybe I could have my voice heard, or at least a few people could hear my opinion," she recounts. Today, her plans are to continue Artivism—art as activism—for the foreseeable future, "showing everyone how to be brave or how to have their own voice out there."

## It's Zombies Versus Coal in East Oakland

For Angelika Soriano, a prospective coal terminal sounded horrifying

ANGELIKA SORIANO AND OTHER YOUTH ACTIVISTS HAVE WORKED TO HALT A PROPOSED COAL TERMINAL. | PHOTO BY LORI EANES

# "IT'S ZOMBIES VERSUS COAL IN EAST OAKLAND"

Angelika Soriano, for *Sierra Club Magazine*

When she was 12, Angelika Soriano came across a YouTube video about climate change. It explained how our planet's rising temperatures correspond with the burning of fossil fuels and warned that humans might not survive this drastic warming. The more she thought about the video, the more anxious she became.

Soriano talked to her friends about climate change, but it didn't seem to worry them much. Her sixth-grade teacher suggested she connect with some youth activists who were fighting a coal terminal proposed for the

**41**

Port of Oakland. A Bay Area developer planned to ship Utah coal to the port and then on to overseas markets.

As Soriano learned more, she started to realize how harmful fossil-fuel-generated air pollutants are to human health, and the effort to block the port became more personal. She and her sister have struggled with the symptoms of asthma, as have many people where she lives in East Oakland. Situated along a corridor with the highest volume of trucking traffic in the Bay Area, East Oakland already has significantly higher levels of air pollution than the rest of the region. "What really scares me the most is the possibility of coal dust flying off the trains and spreading," Soriano says.

For months, she and other youth activists tried to get the developer, Phil Tagami, to meet with them. On the night before Halloween in 2017, she and about 200 other people protested outside Tagami's house. They covered themselves in ashy face paint and fake blood and declared themselves coal zombies. "We got the idea of dressing up as zombies as a way of saying we might be killed by coal," Soriano says.

In November 2018, the city of Oakland canceled the lease for the terminal. Tagami has sued the city twice for blocking the project, but construction hasn't started. At 14, Soriano feels less nervous than she used to. "Becoming an activist," she says, "helped with the stress I felt when I was ... full of worries about the climate."

This article appeared in the September/October 2019 edition with the headline "Zombies Versus Coal."

# "MEET THE BAY AREA TEENS BEHIND THE CLIMATE STRIKES"

Aidyn May Robles, Christopher Soriano, Mariah Lazalde, for *Medium* (excerpt)

## AIDYN, 12

"I got involved when Oakland developer Phil Tagami tried to build a coal terminal and it was going to impact people of color. Having a global climate strike with millions of people tells people in power they need to do something. Our elected officials need to address climate. It can't be just youth. And it's not just Greta Thunberg. There have been other climate activists for decades. Our climate movement has to be intersectional. Even though our main focus is climate — saving the entire earth — we have to focus on indigenous communities, people of color, people from lower [income] communities who don't have a voice. We have to lift them up. 92% of the people who live near refineries and pollution are people of color. That makes them [fossil fuel companies] environmentally racist and environmentally classist."

Christopher Soriano, 12, addresses the crow outside Chevron in San Ramon, CA on September 27.

# CHRISTOPHER SORIANO, 12

"I have asthma. I've had it since I was young, maybe 5 years old. When I was walking to elementary school, I'd get asthma attacks and not be able to breathe. My cousin Angelika has asthma too. Where I live is in a lower income community. On International Ave., you see all these people outside sleeping on the streets. During the wildfires, the people who live on the streets breathe in all that smoke and debris. It's my future that is affected. Not just my generation, but future generations--my kids and my grandchildren. I don't want their lives taken away or made shorter. I don't want to resent myself in the future because I didn't fight for climate justice."

Mariah Lazalde, 15, with their cousin at a protest outside of Chevron in San Ramon, CA on September 27.

# MARIAH LAZALDE, 15

"There isn't any time left. This is a crisis. This is life and death right about now. It makes me both mad and sad. All these people who work at Chevron. They could probably afford to go to school. But I'm fighting for my future. I come from a low income community and we are deeply affected. They [Chevron and the fossil fuel companies] decide to poison our communities because they don't want to poison where they live. It's sad to see people with privilege take advantage and not support us because they won't be affected the way we will. That's why I'm here. I'm taking a lot of risks, like missing school. But the biggest risk is if people don't care."

# "Y IS FOR YOUTH CLIMATE MOVEMENT

Aidyn May Robles, in *Rad American Movements A-Z: Movements and Moments That Demonstrate the Power of the People*

# IS FOR
# YOUTH CLIMATE MOVEMENT

## THE YOUNG LEADERS WORKING TO PROTECT OUR PLANET

"This isn't just climate change anymore—it's climate chaos. This isn't just global warming—it's global catastrophe."
—SAMANTHA MAY, AGE 12, CLIMATE ACTIVIST

CLIMATE CHANGE IS REAL. It's happening. And we need to act—now. That is the core message of the Youth Climate Movement, a growing network of young activists and organizations leading the urgent fight to address and reverse climate change across the United States and around the world.

The majority of scientists agree that human contributions to the greenhouse effect are the root cause of the widespread changes our climate is experiencing. Gases in the atmosphere, such as $CO_2$ and methane, trap heat and then prevent its escape from the planet. This heat causes an increase in surface temperatures—new heat records are being set almost every year. It destabilizes weather patterns around the globe, causing more catastrophic weather events, including hurricanes, extreme storms and rainfall, droughts and heat waves, and resulting floods and forest fires. In the last century alone, global sea levels have risen 6.7 inches—and in the next 100 years, some scientists suggest they could rise as much as 4 feet.

When it comes to taking action on climate change, world leaders tend to debate, deny, or delay. The Youth Climate Movement believes we can't wait. They press forward, leading strikes and marches, confronting their elected officials, and educating their peers about what it will take to ensure a healthy planet and future.

This story is about Americans who want to ensure that we get to have that future. It's told mostly in their voices, because they have something important to say—and we need to listen.

## STANDING ROCK 2014

IN 2014, A LARGE energy corporation wanted to build a huge underground oil pipeline from North Dakota to Illinois. The Dakota Access Pipeline (DAPL) would move half a million barrels of oil per day—and be built directly beneath land, rivers, and burial grounds that are sacred to numerous indigenous Native people, including those living on the Standing Rock Sioux reservation.

While the corporation argued that the pipeline would be safe, the indigenous communities knew the truth: pipeline accidents will inevitably occur, and when they do, the damage can be irreversible, toxic, and deadly. The indigenous people of the region decided to take a stand to protect their land—and it was the youth who took the lead, setting up camps and holding ceremonies.

Using the hashtags #NoDAPL, #mniwiconi, #WaterIsLife, and #StandWithStandingRock, they used social media to spread the message that the pipeline threatened more than the purity of their drinking water—it threatened their health, their culture, and their lives. It was also, they knew, one part of a much larger environmental crisis that their generation is going to inherit—and that their generation must fix. Members of hundreds of Native tribes came to Standing Rock to show solidarity for the people and the earth, and thousands of nonnatives joined the demonstrations too.

"It's important to know that, for Native and indigenous people, this is not just about protecting the climate, the land, and the water so that we can survive. It's deeply connected to who we are—the natural world is our culture. We've been preaching this and valuing these sacred resources since the beginning of time. Due to this, indigenous people should be represented with all climate actions.

"The United States has a long history of extracting natural resources from indigenous lands. We tend to live in rural areas,

which is where most of our reservations or ancestral lands are, and these regions often have the valuable resources they want. When massive oil pipelines are built through indigenous land, it's not only a threat to our environment, but also to our culture. It's a double whammy. This happens throughout the world: wherever resources are being extracted, whether it's oil, water, or trees, you can guarantee an indigenous community lives nearby.

"The Dakota Access Pipeline was being built through unceded Sioux territory. The construction is a direct violation of the Treaty of Fort Laramie of April 29, 1868, also known as the Sioux Treaty, which gave the Sioux people sovereign control over the land.

"The International Indigenous Youth Council started to address this in 2016, armed with the knowledge of our culture and historical contexts. We have to protect our women, our land, our culture. We ask the world, and the corporations, to please honor our treaties, our rights, and our livelihoods.

"We are led by young women and two-spirit people (for us, "two spirit" is someone whose energy encapsulates both masculine and feminine qualities).

"There is a basic understanding among many first nations that our behaviors are the result of actions, thoughts, and prayers that go back seven generations, and that whatever we do, think, and pray about will impact the future seven generations. There is a prophecy among several Native tribes that says seven generations after contact with Europeans there will be a great awakening among Indigenous tribes and allies. Through this awakening people from all over the world would stand together to save Turtle Island [a term for Earth]. *We are the seventh generation. It's happening now—the prophecy is coming true.*

—MEREYA GOETZINGER-BLANCO, MEMBER OF THE INTERNATIONAL INDIGENOUS YOUTH COUNCIL

## JULIANA V. UNITED STATES
### 2015

IN 2015 A GROUP of 21 young people filed a lawsuit against the United States government, asserting that the government's failure to address climate change is a violation of their constitutional rights to life, liberty, and happiness. Climate activist Kelsey Juliana is the named plaintiff on the case, titled *Juliana v. United States*.

"I began climate activism at age 10. It became my life—all my school projects became ways to learn more about climate change. After 8th grade, I filed a case against the state of Oregon, and that's how I began climate litigation. It was a snowball effect: I wanted to hold my school accountable for climate change, then my city, then the state . . . and now I want to hold the federal government accountable.

"When I was in 8th grade, no one else seemed to care about climate change. Now there are 21 of us suing the federal government. We're not scientists or lawyers or experts. We're individual young people being called to collectively take on the greatest challenge of our time. We are trying to hold the systems of power accountable."

—KELSEY JULIANA, AGE 23, LEAD PLAINTIFF

## 2018 YOUTH CLIMATE MARCH

ON JULY 21, 2018, thousands of students across America marched for climate justice in Washington, DC, and in 25 cities around the world. The idea for the first Youth Climate March came from Jamie Margolin, whose inspiration to become a climate activist came, in part, from witnessing the efforts of the Standing Rock activists.

"For a long time, I was just a kid who learned about climate change. I cared about it, but it was so scary to me. I didn't know what to do with that fear. Whenever a news story about climate change came on, I would turn it off. That all changed with the 2016 election.

"I realized that I had to take this fear and channel it into something productive. I watched a documentary about the Standing Rock activists, and was so moved by the way these indigenous youth from a really disadvantaged community have managed to start this international movement. I thought if they could do it under those circumstances, I could do it too.

"During the summer of 2017, I had the idea: What if there was a youth climate march? I imagined a big event that would put the world's eyes on youth climate activism. I posted on Instagram and got a few responses from young people who wanted to help, from across the country. We formed a team and for an entire year we organized, and a year later, on July 21, 2018, we had the Youth Climate March on Washington and in 25 cities around the world."

"We're called Zero Hour because this is 'zero hour' to work on climate change. Anything other than immediate action now is denying it and dooming life on earth. There's no gray area on survival—either we survive this or we don't."

—JAMIE MARGOLIN, AGE 18, FOUNDER OF ZERO HOUR

IN AUGUST 2018, a 15-year-old Swedish teenager named Greta Thunberg began her skolstrejk för klimatet (school strike for climate) when she started skipping school to demand action on climate change by protesting outside of the Swedish Parliament building. She quickly inspired young people around the world to do the same. On March 15, 2019, more than one million students in 125 countries went on strike to bring attention to climate change. In New York City, 12-year-old Alexandria Villaseñor began striking outside of the United Nations headquarters every Friday.

"I was visiting family in Davis, California, in November of 2018 when the Paradise Fire broke out. I was an hour away from the fire, but we had the worst air quality in the world at the time. The smoke was so terrible, it was seeping into the house.

"I made the connection that climate change is fueling California's wildfires, and making them more extreme. California's fire season is all year round now. I started researching climate change and paying attention to the United Nations Climate Change Conference. I was hoping that world leaders would come to an agreement to reduce greenhouse gas emissions by 2030, but when they didn't, I got really mad.

"Then I saw Greta Thunberg speak. On December 14, 2018, I started my own school strike for climate at the United Nations headquarters in New York City. I've been on strike for 22 weeks now (as of yesterday). Students all over the world are taking direct action, going out into the streets every Friday to strike. We ARE starting to make change.

"I want to get climate education into schools so we can start learning the facts. Climate change is not an opinion—it's science."

—ALEXANDRIA VILLASEÑOR, AGE 13, FOUNDER OF EARTH UPRISING

YOUTH VS. APOCALYPSE IS a diverse group of young climate justice activists working together to lift the voices of youth—especially youth of color—and to fight for a livable climate and a sustainable, just world. In 2019 several members of Youth vs. Apocalypse joined members of the climate justice group the Sunrise Movement in a visit to the office of California Senator Dianne Feinstein. Their tense interaction went viral when Senator Feinstein seemed to dismiss their concerns about climate change and the Green New Deal, an ambitious legislative plan to address climate change and create new jobs.

"I got started with climate activism when I was 13 years old and I was invited to an action by a friend. We went to deliver a letter to a local developer who was trying to build a coal terminal through my neighborhood in West Oakland, California. It would have severely impacted the lives and health of people that I know and love.

"To be honest, before I got involved in the climate movement, I disregarded it. I saw it as a 'white issue'—like, who has time to save the rainforests when black people are being shot by police every day? Then I realized that climate injustice is rooted in our culture of greed and exploitation. That coal terminal awakened me to the reality of the climate movement.

"Our culture is realizing that climate change is really important. People my age are actually caring, and wanting to do something about it. We've seen people in power implement plans that haven't worked. We have that whole story behind us, and we can look to the past to analyze how best to move forward."

**—ISRA CLARKE, AGE 16, YOUTH VS. APOCALYPSE**

"I like to go for a straightforward approach when I give speeches to grown-ups: I tell them climate change is gonna kill us. How can we let it happen? We have to let the Green New Deal pass. I spoke with representatives from the Environmental Protection Agency. I told them they need to protect the youth.

"I feel empowered: when I'm speaking, it's the adults looking to learn from us about what they can do to help.

"A lot of people say I should be a politician. Even my mom said she thinks I'm going to be president. But I don't want to be in charge of a group of people—I want to be with people, guiding them instead of directing them."

**—SAMANTHA MAY, AGE 12, YOUTH VS. APOCALYPSE**

## Y ALSO FOR . . .

**YELLOW POWER:** A term used in the 1960s and '70s to refer to the new Asian American civil rights movement.

**YIPPIES:** The members of the Youth International Party, founded in 1967, an offshoot of the free speech and antiwar movements.

**YOUNG LORDS:** A national organization, inspired by the Black Panthers, that championed liberation, self-determination, and justice for Puerto Rican and Latinx people in the late 1960s to mid-1970s.

# WARRIORS FOR JUSTICE
## OP-ED

# "THESE 10 OP-EDS FROM YOUTH CLIMATE STRIKERS EXPLAIN THEIR NEED TO TAKE ACTION"

Angelika Soriano excerpt from *Sunrise Movement* on *Medium* (March 18, 2019)

On March 15, students in over 120 countries skipped school, but it wasn't just for fun. It was part of a worldwide coordinated effort to call attention to the most pressing threat to their generation — climate change. Read why these ten teens cut class and how they perceive their future on a warming planet.

Read why these ten teens cut class and how they perceive their future on a warming planet...

**full article available on** *Medium.com*
https://medium.com/sunrisemvmt/these-10-op-eds-from-youth-climate-strikers-explain-their-need-to-take-action-c2891e983a6f

# Angelika S., age 14, Oakland, CA (8th grade, Youth vs. Apocalypse)

I am participating in the Climate Strike Friday because if we don't do anything about climate change, it's going to slowly kill us.

When I learned about climate change through the internet, it terrified me. This made me feel helpless and hopeless. This fear was kept in the back of my head until I was introduced to Warriors for Justice, a student-led club, and No Coal in Oakland, which was a campaign opposing a developer named Phil Tagami who's building a coal terminal in West Oakland. This brought me relief because I was working for a cause and trying my best to create a change.

But this was the start of our battle. Climate change is real. Have you seen the wildfires from last year? We had to wear masks to even step foot outside of our home because of how toxic the air was. This is the reality we're living in.

Imagine the future for you, for me, the youth, your kids, your grandkids, and the animals roaming now. What will happen to all of them? Will they live up to the age of 30, without wearing a mask to go outside? This is why we need to fight together. Will you be part of the change, or watch our future perish?

# WARRIORS FOR JUSTICE
## SPEECHES

# ENVIRONMENTAL PROTECTION AGENCY "LISTENING SESSION" (FEBRUARY 28, 2018)

Aidyn May Robles Testifying

# Everything Is At Stake
# Because Of Coal (Testimony)

This world we live in, at this very moment, is all we have. It breaks us kids' hearts to know that the people who are supposed to protect our environment are destroying it. Children like us have to fear the government because of what they are doing. Is the world supposed to be like that? Should we fear the people that should protect us? Will we ever be safe again? Why is the EPA doing this? Shouldn't they protect our environment? All of these questions form in our heads when we think of this crisis. Children and people in parts of the world have to wear a mask to step outside! Should our country follow their lead?

Our leaders are putting our health at risk for what? Money. Passing coal through Oakland will bring wealth to them, and death to us. So I'd like to share mine and many others' opinions so I can say something and make a difference. We kids are trying to help our planet by reducing the amount of pollution polluting our clean air. Coal is a cheap form of fuel full of profits for the rich and toxins for the poor. It causes black lungs, cancer, asthma attacks, it causes so many things that risk our Earth, our only home. So many animals are going extinct because of us humans. We should be protecting them, not harming these animals.

Climate change like this takes a while to be noticeable, maybe thirty to forty years. It shouldn't have been so hot in Oakland last September, but it was. And things like this keep happening to the point children have to speak up. We don't want our Earth to die like this. We don't want to die knowing our own EPA put our lives at risk for money. This is happening across the world, but if we stop our excessive pollution, it can make a positive difference. Even if it is just us.

Big things start little. Us kids started off little, but look at us now-standing up for what is right. We are here to make a difference, we want to live. We want our children to be safe and healthy. I want to know my grandchildren will lead long and healthy lives. Our future generation is at stake. Many of you have children, right? Don't you want them and their family safe? Don't you care about their health?

If we keep this up, we will be at stake. If we keep increasing global warming, we are putting everything and everyone we love down. If we do terrible things that our officials believe we should, humanity won't last. Everything we do now is leading to something big. Outcomes will form different paths to be taken- they all depend on now.

Just because we are humans does not negate the fact that we can go extinct, because we can just like any other species. And, I can not believe anyone would want their bloodline to die. That is why we must start now, by not letting coal destroy us. Because as I said, big things start little. Huge changes were once just a group of people wanting to make a difference. And forthcoming changes are us kids wanting a better future.

This speech leads down to what I want- what we want, as children. We don't want coal in Oakland, or anywhere. What we do want is clean air, because clean air leads to a better future. And, we must have responsible and aware leaders if we want a better future. So please listen carefully to what we say, because it does affect everyone. It affects wildlife, it affects me, it affects us, it affects you. And, I am sure you would like to live past eighty, maybe enough to meet your great grandchildren.

I understand we all have different opinions. And since I have heard yours, I would like you to listen to mine. And, I hope you have, because that would make me extremely happy.

This is the only Earth there is, so we must protect it. We have to let Earth breathe.

# CalSTRS LISTENING SESSION
Aidyn May Robles (May 8, 2019)

When you become a teacher, you sign up to not only care for children, but to educate the future leaders of society. To find out that the people I have spent most of my life with are funding to pour toxins into my future is a real slap to the face. It's a message telling the youth that you don't really care for our future, and it contradicts exactly what a teacher is. It's a message telling me and all other students that we can't trust the adults who prepare us for the rest of our lives...All I can say is, stop funding to destroy my future.

Hello, I am Aidyn and I am a 7th grader from Oakland. I came all the way from Oakland and skipped a very special day in my school called Service Day, where the sole purpose of that day is to give to our community, but I decided that instead of focusing on just my community, I'll take this opportunity to save our only planet. I've already spoken to the Environmental Protection Agency as to why fossil fuels and coal are destructive for our environment. I have spoken to Nancy Pelosi's staff as to why they should invest in the Green New Deal. Then I went to Dianne Feinstein's office with about 20 youth to encourage her to support the Green New Deal. After her response, I helped organise a youth climate strike and we went back to her office with nearly 2,000 student strikers. I've talked to many adults and people in power and elected officials, but why am I constantly hit with a brick wall? Why are me and all the youth here not taken seriously?

The youth are always told we are ignorant. We apparently know nothing about anything. But as soon as we fight for a future, as soon as we have the knowledge to protect our future, we're suddenly too young to know. We are too young to know anything. Too young to save ourselves. Too young to uplift our voices. Too young to stand up for all the youth around the world. Suddenly, we are too young to live. And guess what? We aren't. And I have a special message, especially for you.

You should already know this, but I'm here to put this in perspective. When you become a teacher, you sign up to not only care for children, but to educate the future leaders of society. But, to find out that teacher retirement funds are being used to pour toxins into my future is a real slap to the face. It's a message telling the youth that you don't really care for our future, and it contradicts exactly what a teacher is. It's a message telling me and all other students that we can't trust the adults who prepare us for the rest of our lives. Every day you spent in the classroom was a waste of time if you really plan on erasing the future of all the students you taught.

Companies that use fossil fuels are not a worthy place to invest money into. This is our last chance to save our planet, this is our very last resort. And we aren't just here to discuss this, we are here to tell you to take action now. Consider the words coming out of my mouth as not only a message from me, but make this a message from the future. That if you don't divest now, the youth will be staring at you from the future. They will be wondering why you decided to fund fossil fuels. We will be wondering why you decided to fund the end of the human race, why you let my city sink, and why you let the polar bears die?! This isn't just climate change. This is climate chaos. This isn't just global warming anymore, this is global catastrophe. Keep this in mind; the future has its eyes on you.

# OAKLAND PUBLIC EDUCATION FUND GALA

Christopher Soriano, Aidyn May Robles, Sophia Lopez Garcia

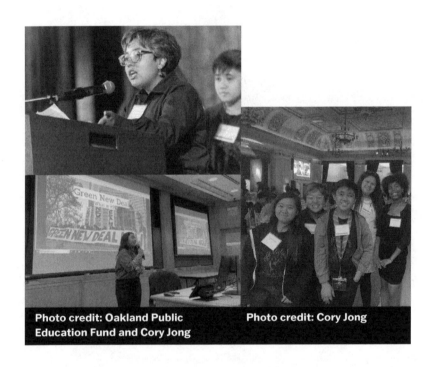

Photo credit: Oakland Public
Education Fund and Cory Jong

Photo credit: Cory Jong

## CHRISTOPHER SORIANO

Hello everyone, my name is Christopher. Thank you so much for inviting us here today; it is truly an honor to be here. I'm a 7th grader at Urban Promise Academy, and I'm part of a youth-led club at school, called Warriors for Justice. I first joined Warriors for Justice when I was a 6th grader, and because both of my cousins were part of the club. Angeline is a founding member of Warriors for Justice, and Angelika was one of the main presenters of the conference at Harvard.

We first heard about the Alumni of Color Conference thanks to César Cruz and Homies Empowerment. César is an alum at Harvard University, and César was the main reason we knew about the conference and were encouraged to turn in the proposal to Harvard that got accepted. Without César, we probably wouldn't have even known about the conference in the first place, and we probably wouldn't be here right now at this gala. The A to Z fund was also another reason why we were able to fund our trip to Boston. Our grant was accepted and we were able to get the $1500 for the trip, along with donations from our community and families.

Going to Harvard University was a huge confidence boost for me. Before I went to Harvard, I didn't think of myself as an organizer, but after the trip, I felt like I had the power to do so because I'd just presented at an Ivy League University. I stand here today as a youth activist who wants to fight for their future. Going to Harvard also enhanced my presentation skills as an overall student at Urban Promise Academy. The practice of presenting there prepared me to speak at bigger events like this gala, talking to the press, doing media, going to CalSTRS board meetings, and co-facilitating a meeting with Fiona Ma, the state treasurer, and MCing rallies.

# SOPHIA LOPEZ GARCIA

Hello, I'm Sophia. I'm 13 years old. I am in the 8th grade at Urban Promise Academy. I was 12 when I went to Harvard. It was my first time on the other side of the country. The only universities I've ever visited are here in the Bay Area or in California, such as Cal, Laney, Cal State East Bay and Cal State LA. How did going to Harvard change my identity? I get nervous speaking in front of people. All the time. I forget how to speak. Going to Harvard and having the opportunity to speak to a group of people about climate change helped me with my public speaking skills. It also gave me a confidence boost in presenting and talking with adults. As a member with ADD, or attention deficit disorder without the hyperactive, being a Warriors for Justice member helps me stay more focused and responsible with my time management. Having ADD, I didn't know how to read until the 3rd grade. In 6th grade, I was the third highest in reading Lexile. Warriors for Justice members are scholars because we prioritize our academics. Our school slogan is "Developing Scholars, Warriors, and Artists." Our club helps us develop skills in these areas. We are also the most diverse club in the school, in terms of race, gender, sexuality, disability, age, and not only includes all three grades, but we have alumni that keep coming back year after year. I've been raised to give back to the community, and I hope you will too, by donating to the A to Z fund.

## AIDYN MAY ROBLES

Hello, my name is Aidyn, and I am 12 years old. I am an 8th grader at Urban Promise Academy. I was 12 when I first flew in a plane. And not only did I fly on a plane, I flew to Harvard. Our social justice group at our middle school is called Warriors for Justice, and a group of us had the opportunity to fly to Boston, Massachusetts, and speak at the Harvard Graduate School of Education. We had our own session during the Alumni of Color Conference, where we talked about how Warriors for Justice started, and how we got to where we are. We started from talking about the sex trafficking that happens in our community and across the United States, to fighting for climate justice for the planet and our future. We discussed community violence and also went to big politicians' offices, such as Dianne Feinstein and Nancy Pelosi. We came from organizing 2,000 students for the March 15th Climate Strike with Youth vs. Apocalypse to organizing 10,000 people for the September 20th Global Climate Strike.

But where did this confidence come from? How could we become so close with people we met from our school? How did a bunch of pre-teens suddenly become as close as family with other people their age? Simple. We slept in the same room. For four nights. And we also had snowball fights in the middle of the street, which doesn't happen in Oakland often, or like, at all. We stayed at a community house, with organizers from Blackyard Arts. We were introduced to them by Carolyn and Greg, who are organizers with Youth vs. Apocalypse. By staying at a community house with Ashley and Mama Linda, we found a second home. Not everyone gets to cook a dish from their culture for anybody. Not everyone trusts someone enough to eat the food they've cooked for them. Not everyone dances to meme music with each other, or plays roblox till 4 am, or has a mochi ice cream party, or eats pizza constantly, or gets to go to an authentic Chinese restaurant with Sifu Mai and Sifu Andrea. But we got to do all that, and more! And that wasn't even part of the conference!

At the conference, we were the only youth our age that got to present. We talked about the dynamics of our school and what living in Oakland is like, since not everyone that was there knew Oakland's environment. We talked about sex trafficking and the violence that happens in our community. We talked about No Coal in Oakland, where a developer named Phil Tagami is trying to sue the city of Oakland to build a coal terminal in West Oakland. We talked about the Green New Deal, how we need that for a better future. We also spoke about the teacher's strike, and how people we knew were on the picket line at our school, while we were presenting at Harvard.

But how were we able to go? Who were the people that made this possible for us? The first person was César Cruz from Homies Empowerment. He's the one who told us about the Alumni of Color Conference, and said we should submit a proposal. Then we have everyone who donated to us, the people who funded our trip. Including the people from A-Z Fund, who funded most of the cost for our airfare. And all the people we met in Cambridge and Boston. From random Lyft drivers, to V, who is from Oakland and is the new director for the Harvard Graduate School of Education. And I want to thank the members of Warriors for Justice, the people at Harvard and the people who held down the picket lines at our school. I want to thank all the people who believed in us, and everyone in this crowd.

We are the future, and our voices should be listened to. And despite the fact that this speech should be focused on our trip to Harvard and how A-Z funded us, I want to bring up the fact that the Earth is dying. We have to take drastic measures in order to save it, since we are the only ones that can. And also that's the main focus of our group. I'll also end this like I end most of my speeches. The future has its eyes on you.

We'd like to close with a unity clap, in the tradition of the United Farmworkers, a labor union of Chicano, or Mexican, and Filipino farmworkers who started in the 1960s. You may have heard of César Chavez and Dolores Huerta, but have you also heard of Larry Itliong and Philip Vera Cruz? Since people didn't speak the same language, they created a way to show unity and action. In Tagalog, "Isang" means "one," and "Bagsak" means "fall or down." The unity clap is personally important to me because I myself am Filipino. We close with the unity clap with "Isang Bagsak" to show that when one of us falls, we all fall, and when one of us rises, we all rise. The clapping of our hands symbolizes a heartbeat. We start off clapping our hands slowly, and start to speed up, then I'll say "Isang Bagsak," and we'll stop all together on a huge clap. So, are you ready? Okay.

# HARVARD GRADUATE SCHOOL OF EDUCATION
Alumni of Color Conference (March 2019)

# Warriors for Justice Community Report Back

Harvard Alumni of Color Conference
Blackyard Arts in Camden
Wah Lum Kung Fu, USA in Malden
Harvard Arts in Education Class

## Join us at Homies Empowerment

7631 MacArthur Blvd.
Sat. 3/30
4:30 - 6:30

We hope to also discuss youth activism to learn from each other, and share our recent work on the Youth Climate Strike in SF on 3/15 to support the Green New Deal

71

# 49ERS FOUNDATION DR. HARRY EDWARDS FOLLOW YOUR BLISS AWARD, MIDDLE SCHOOL TEACHER OF THE YEAR (2021)

Mx. Cory Jong (2021)

Good afternoon! Thank you to the 49ers Foundation, Jesse Lovejoy, Dr. John York, Extra Yard for Teachers, Micron, and Dr. Harry Edwards, for this honor. Congratulations to my fellow award recipients.

It seems fitting that this Dr. Harry Edwards Follow Your Bliss award is coming from the 49ers Foundation, because when I was growing up, the 49ers brought a lot of joy to my parents, and Bill Walsh, Joe Montana, and Jerry Rice were essentially a part of my childhood. My parents were small business owners in Berkeley, and owned Winner's Circle Tennis and Winner's Circle Systems. They rarely took a day off or went on vacation, but one thing they did to brighten their weekend was watch 49ers games together. That, and play tennis. I want to thank my mom, Helen, my sister, Kristin, and my aunt, Nancy, who encouraged me to apply for this award, and my family for their unconditional love and support. I know that my dad is smiling at this moment as an ancestor, along with my Pau Pau Lizzie, Gung Gung Francis, and Pau Pau May.

As a child, going with my grandparents to community gatherings, my family modeled for me the importance of forming a connection with others in order to have an impact on the world we live in, through their involvement in founding the Berkeley Chinese Community Church, the Oakland Chinatown Chamber of Commerce, Bok Sen restaurant, and their leadership in our family associations, the Buddhist Temple, and UC Berkeley Chinese Alumni Association.

For this reason, I have always participated in clubs and organizations. In the late '90s, I was trained in mass-line organizing, and helped start an organization known as Pro-People Youth, Kabataang maka-Bayan, as well as API organizations at UCLA. The work of KmB is influenced by the tradition of organizations like the Black Panther Party (BPP), originally known as the Black Panther Party for Self-Defense, and anti-imperialist organizing in solidarity with the movement in the Philippines. From this perspective, to build a movement, you need to educate, organize, and mobilize.

I became an educator in order to organize youth. As an educator and community organizer, I believe, as June Jordan says, "We are the ones we've been waiting for." One of my mentors, Yuri Kochiyama, shared with me in the late 1990s, a quote by Frantz Fanon that continues to guide me: "Each generation must, out of relative obscurity, discover its mission, fulfill it, or betray it." I begin each school year posing this challenge to my students. My mission is to support youth in discovering their passions and sense of purpose, and to organize youth to find their voice and be agents of change. I also believe that, as I learned in my teaching credential program, that "they don't care what you know until they know that you care." I go above and beyond for my students and their families because I want them to know how much I care, and because as youth, they hold the future in their hands.

One of the reasons I am a middle school teacher is because I vividly recall my years of puberty, going to school in Richmond, when I felt moments of loneliness, confusion, and isolation. It is the transitional stage of development from childhood to adolescence. Having teachers and mentors who believed in me, supported me, encouraged me, helped me build my capacity, and provided access to resources, was pivotal for me in finding my place and purpose in this world, and now it is my turn to plant the seeds and cultivate the next generation.

As a youth, the richest learning opportunities and teachable moments came from relationships with adults who were willing to model vulnerability as a strength, shared stories and wisdom that had been passed on to them, took time to listen, helped me gain knowledge of self, gave me their time and attention, were emotionally regulated, modeled patience, and provided unconditional love. As a middle school student in Richmond, and as a graduate of Berkeley High School, I was also challenged to think critically and encouraged to build knowledge of self by studying history. My students say that they appreciate how I "keep it real," help them understand the world around them by addressing the current events impacting us today, and provide them with opportunities to engage in the issues that matter to them and express how they are feeling. When it comes to climate justice education, we need to prepare students faced with catastrophic climate chaos. Students need to be prepared to fight for their future. When it comes to addressing anti-Black racism and building interracial solidarity, students need to be able to ask difficult questions, challenge the world as we know it, and have space for healing and action. When it comes to helping youth understand what democracy looks like and their role in the future of our community, state, nation, and world, we can't afford to wait.

In closing, this award is a reflection of all of the collaborative teams I work with at Urban Promise Academy, where we develop scholars, artists, and warriors. This award also reflects my participation in Agency by Design Oakland, the OUSD Ethnic Studies cohort, SFJazz partnership, Himalayan Yoga of Joy sangha, and my work with the adult advisory board of Youth vs. Apocalypse. Tú eres mi otro yo, you are my other me.

The resources will support my students, classroom, and school that I serve in the Fruitvale district of East Oakland, as well as the youth organizers in Warriors for Justice. I hope to make my family, community, and the 49ers Foundation proud. In the tradition of the Filipino movement, I'll close with a chant that I learned in my early years as an organizer: Makibaka, Huwagmatakot! Dare to struggle, don't be afraid. Thank you.

**JOIN US TO CELEBRATE OUR 2021**
**FOLLOW YOUR BLISS AWARD RECIPIENTS**

Binh Dao     Cory Jong     Michele Lamons-Raiford

Brittney-Lynn Filimoehala-Egan     Emmanuel Stewart

**Tuesday, June 1ˢᵗ 2021**
**4:30 PM PT - 5:30 PM PT**

RSVP at 49ers.com/followyourbliss

# WARRIORS FOR JUSTICE
## MURALS

# "RISE FOR CLIMATE, JOBS, & JUSTICE" (SEPTEMBER 12, 2018)

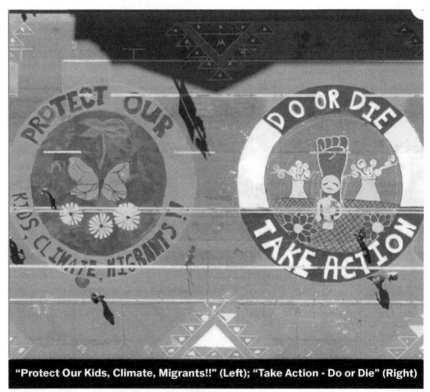

"Protect Our Kids, Climate, Migrants!!" (Left); "Take Action - Do or Die" (Right)

Angelika was the lead artist on our first street murals in 2018. We were trained by David Solnit and the Climate Justice Street Mural Project. 55 groups painted climate solutions murals over five blocks surrounding San Francisco Civic Center Plaza.

Photo Cred: Bunker | Survival Media Agency

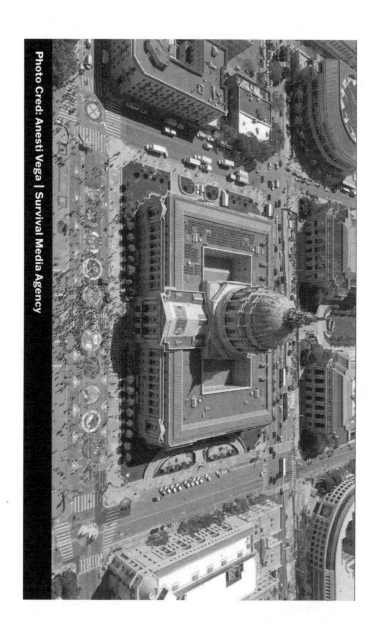

# "CLIMATE JUSTICE NOW! CLIMATE ACTION 4 ALL" (MAY 3, 2019)

Youth vs. Apocalypse and Warriors for Justice hosted a Fruitvale Block Party for Climate Justice, on May 3, 2019. Santiago Olin was the lead artist as a 6th grader. The left side of the mural represents a sustainable, healthy future, and the right side represents wildfires and climate chaos. The text says Climate Justice Now! Climate Action 4 All.

# "THE YOUTH ARE WATCHING—NO COAL IN OAKLAND" (NOVEMBER 7, 2019)

Field trip with 6th-8th grade students from UPA
Mariah Lazalde and Isha Clarke co-emceed

# "COMMUNITY VOICE IS A PRIORITY - OAKLAND CLIMATE STRIKE" (JANUARY 17, 2020)

# "LXS VIDXS NEGRXS IMPORTAN, BLACK LIVES MATTER MURAL" (JUNE 17, 2020)
## Black Lives Matter Mural Project at the Fruitvale Village

This mural was created in July of 2020, only a few months into the quarantine, in response to the murder of George Floyd and Breonna Taylor. This project was initiated by Crystal Barajas Barr (Urban Promise Academy art teacher and GSA-Rainbow Club liaison) and Adrianna Alvarez (United for Success Academy art teacher), supported by Warriors for Justice, Val Lizarraga (former UPA / La Clinica Health Educator), Inés Ixierda, Vick Montano, and Oree Originol. Located in Fruitvale Village next to Fruitvale BART, this mural was part of a series that included "Two Spirits for Black Lives" (Dos Espiritus Por Las Vidas Negras - Stolen Land, Stolen People), "Black Trans Lives Matter" (Lxs Vidxs Negrxs Trans Importan), and a memorial piece for Erik Salgado and Oscar Grant on the side of the La Clinica de la Raza, on E.12$^{th}$ St. and 35$^{th}$ Avenue. All of this was part of the public protest art and call for Black Lives Matter that occurred around the nation during the summer of 2020, and locally, Unity Council coordinated panels for local businesses in Fruitvale.

The Warriors for Justice mural was designed by Aidyn May Robles, and says Black Lives Matter in Spanish, with the use of "X" to be gender non-conformming. "Tu Lucha Es Mi Lucha," "Your Struggle is My Struggle" shows Black and Brown solidarity, the rainbow lettering and fingernails show LGBTQ+ solidarity, the butterflies represent migrant rights and the cempasuchiles honor the ancestors. On the left, two portraits include the names of Black people murdered by police.

Lead artist: Aidyn May Robles
Initiating artists:
Crystal Barajas Barr, Urban Promise Academy
Adrianna Alvarez, United for Success Academy
Partnering organizations:
Gender Sexuality Alliance - Rainbow Club

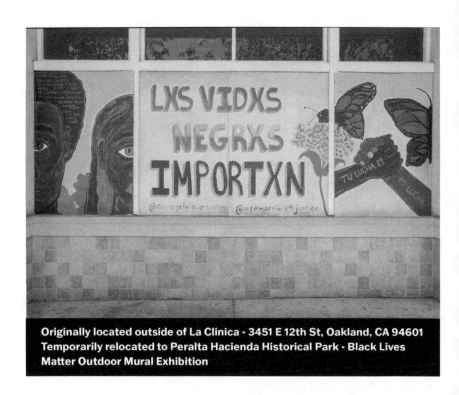

**Originally located outside of La Clinica · 3451 E 12th St, Oakland, CA 94601 Temporarily relocated to Peralta Hacienda Historical Park · Black Lives Matter Outdoor Mural Exhibition**

# "CHOOSE DEMOCRACY STREET MURAL" (OCTOBER 29, 2020)

Leading up to the Presidential Election of 2020, Warriors for Justice was invited to participate in a mural project: "Choose Democracy: Stop a Coup," led by East Point Peace Academy and the Climate Justice Street Mural Project. Specifically, we asked ourselves: what does democracy look like for youth? It is intersectional, involves all power to the people, and organizing! Sunflowers represent climate justice and the organizing work we do with Youth vs. Apocalypse. This is the time for youth to take action. The black background and yellow lettering of the lettering represent the movement for Black Lives (Black Lives Matter & #SayHerName). The background is a rainbow for LGBTQ+ rights and the fingernail for Transgender rights. The fist represents the legacy of the movement, the strength, and power of working together. The butterfly represents migrant rights. The cempasúchiles honor Día de Los Muertos, the ancestors, and those lost to violence. The purple roses represent an end to the sex trafficking of womyn and children (Af3IRM Purple Rose campaign and transnational feminism) and is also similar to our Warriors for Justice logo, part of our origins.

A photo of the youth who participated, ages 6 - 18, including newcomer students and students with disabilities. We were also supported by current and former staff from Urban Promise Academy, alumni, and family members, to make this project happen.

# "CalSTRS STOP LINE 3 MURAL"
# (FEBRUARY 27, 2021)

**Art designed by Christopher Soriano**
**Photo credit: Earth Guardians Bay Area**

# "DEFUND DESTRUCTION, FUND OUR FREEDOM!" (JUNE 26, 2021)

# "HONOR OUR EARTH! CALSTRS DIVEST, DEFUND LINE 3" (SEPTEMBER 3, 2021)

Art designed by Amaru Preciado-Cruz

# RESOURCES

## Music Videos on Climate Justice

**No One Is Disposable featuring Coco Peila, Dulce C. Arias, RyanNicole, Lizbeth Ibarra, Katerina Gaines, Sarah Goody**
https://www.youtube.com/watch?v=q9905wtDb_U

**This Is The Time: Youth Vs Apocalypse ft Raka Dun, Alphabet Rockers and Destiny Arts**
https://www.youtube.com/watch?v=Fj-uFN-Etql&t=1s

**Where's The Money At?: Youth Vs Apocalypse ft Rudy Kalma, Destiny Arts Center, and Warriors for Justice**
https://www.youtube.com/watch?v=L9BK16pT_Mc

## Resources on Climate Justice

**Youth vs Apocalypse**
https://www.youthvsapocalypse.org

**Sunrise Movement**
https://www.sunrisemovement.org

**Fridays for the Future**
https://fridaysforfuture.org/

**Survival Media Agency**
http://survivalmediaagency.com/

**How women and girls are leading the way to the end of the fossil fuel era | Antonia Juhasz | TEDxCU**
https://www.youtube.com/watch?v=XQpFEquUC7U

**Angelica Perkins Poem at Climate One Event**
https://www.youtube.com/watch?v=m9NCpR1UGh8

**'Choose Democracy, Stop a Coup:' Guerilla Street Mural in Oakland**
https://www.commondreams.org/views/2020/11/02/choose-democracy-stop-coup-guerilla-street-mural-oakland

**Street Murals to Glasgow: "Defund Climate Chaos!"**
https://www.commondreams.org/views/2021/11/01/street-murals-glasgow-defund-climate-chaos

**"Youth on every continent united in strikes to demand climate action"**
https://newsela.com/read/youth-climate-protest/id/57517/

# Resources on Solidarity Organizations

**Homies Empowerment**
http://www.homiesempowerment.com/

**Af3IRM**
https://af3irm.org/af3irm/

**BoomShake**
http://www.boomshakemusic.com/

**Abundant Beginnings**
http://abundantbeginnings.org/

**Anti Police-Terror Project**
https://www.antipoliceterrorproject.org/

**Sogorea Te' Land Trust**
https://sogoreate-landtrust.org/

**Oakland LGBTQ Center**
https://www.oaklandlgbtqcenter.org/

**BlackYard Arts**
Instagram: @blackyardarts

# Suggested Films on Oakland and/or Social Movements

**International Boulevard: A Documentary by Devika Productions**
https://www.youtube.com/watch?v=VYMWn4JsO00&t=1s

**All Power to the People: The Black Panther Party and Beyond by Lee Lew Lee**
https://www.youtube.com/watch?v=pKvE6_s0jy0

**All Power to the People: Black Panthers at 50 by Oakland Museum of California**
https://www.youtube.com/watch?v=0lhzbA6lHTQ
https://museumca.org/black-panthers-video-playlist

**Displaced by Youth Beat**
https://youthbeat.org/displaced

**We Are the Dream: The Kids of the Oakland MLK Oratorical Fest**
https://www.hbo.com/documentaries/we-are-the-dream

**Yuri Kochiyama: Passion for Justice by Rea Tajiri**
https://www.imdb.com/title/tt0268768/

## Three Films by Peter Nicks (available for purchase online)

**Homeroom**
https://www.imdb.com/title/tt13622168/

**The Force**
https://www.imdb.com/title/tt6159518/

**The Waiting Room**
https://www.imdb.com/title/tt1618399/
This site has a description of all three films
http://openhood.org/about-us/#about

# Resources on Education

**Urban Promise Academy**
http://www.urbanpromiseacademy.org/

**SFJazz - Jazz in the Middle**
https://www.sfjazz.org

**Agency by Design Oakland**
http://www.abdoakland.org/

**OUSD Ethnic Studies Cohort**
https://www.ousd.org/Page/20149

**Abolitionist Teaching Network**
https://abolitionistteachingnetwork.org/

**Project Zero**
http://www.pz.harvard.edu/
http ://www.pz.harvard.edu/thinking-routines

**Teachers for Social Justice**
https://t4sj.org/

# READING GUIDE

Think about themes or ideas around challenges or successes that you and/or your group has had. What would you like to share with others who might be starting social justice groups, other youth who want to become more involved, and future-casting ideas or dreams for where the work might go?

## Poetry

Choose a poem as inspiration for a writing activity. If there is a local community event or Oratorical Festival in your area, we encourage you to share your piece as spoken word.

## Social Studies

### Civic engagement

- Write an op-ed to a local publication about an issue that matters to you

- Find an action in your area to get involved in an issue that matters to you

- Find an organization and attend a local community event

- Choose a speech as inspiration for writing your own public comment or keynote address

## Biography research

Use one of the interviews or articles featured in the book to write biographies about warriors

- What issues matter to this person?

- What actions did this person take to address the issues that matter to them?

- What connections can you make to this person's life?

## Film resource

Watch a film from the resource list and facilitate a discussion

# Art

## See-Think-Wonder

Choose a photo to discuss:

- What do you see?

- What does this make you think about?

- What does it make you wonder about?

## Street murals

Create your own street mural design, addressing an issue that is important to you. Use the examples from the book as a starting point.

Often, street murals will have a slogan or phrase, with lettering in a circle around the outside.

Prepare for the mural. Think about the symbols, colors, and message you want to communicate. Feel free to do research and draw from inspiration and images you find online. Make sure your mural is not too complex, since street murals are often painted in one session over the course of a few hours.

## If you are going to paint it on the ground, you will need the following materials:

- Chalk
- String
- Pole or stick
- Tempura paint (temporary)
- Small containers
- Brushes
- Water
- Large container/s for a cleaning station (tupperware or the type you use to soak dishes) - if you have 2 or 3, you can use this to soak and clean, going from dirty to clean
- Rags
- Ladder (optional)
- Drone camera (optional)

## For the day of the street mural:

- Have your design ready, printed out, if possible, or an
- image that can be shared on people's phones to work from as a guide
- To create the circle, attach the string on one end to the pole or stick
- Attach chalk to the other end of the string
- Use the chalk to create a circle
- For lettering, count out the number of space for the number of

letters, and write the message
- Outline the letters to make them into bubble letters
- Chalk the design
- Swatch the colors on the design
- Prep the tempera paint by pouring the colors into small containers, and add a little water to stretch the amount of paint needed
- Get a team of volunteers to help paint the mural
- Take a photo once you are finished, since the mural is temporary and washable
- If you have a ladder handy, you can get a more elevated view of the mural
- If you have a drone camera, you can get an aerial view of the mural

**Another alternative is to paint your designs on canvas. For this you will need:**

- Canvas
- Base coat (Oops paint from a home improvement store)
- Chalk to sketch the design
- Acrylic paint (permanent)
- Brushes
- Water
- Large container/s for a cleaning station (tupperware or the type you use to soak dishes) - if you have 2 or 3, you can use this to soak and clean, going from dirty to clean
- Rags

# ACKNOWLEDGMENTS

We would like to start by acknowledging that the land we are on is stolen land occupied under settler colonialism. Specifically, being based in the Fruitvale district of East Oakland, we are in the territory of Huichin, and we thank the Confederated Villages of Lisjan, Ohlone, Muwekma, and Chochenyo nations, the successors of the historic and sovereign Verona Band of Alameda County. We stand in solidarity, and show respect and remembrance, as you continue to advance the struggle to rematriate the land, resist, thrive, defend, and to sustain sacred traditions, life, and culture.

We dedicate this book to our family and loved ones who have passed, our ancestors, and to future generations. You inspire us and give us strength.

Thank you to our founding members. Warriors for Justice wouldn't be here without you and the passion you showed for social justice. Thank you to all of the members and youth who have participated with us over the years. Shout-out to Samy Ramirez-Mata and current 2021-2022 members for holding it down and continuing the work.

Thank you to our families. Without your nourishment, love, and support, we would not be who we are. Thank you to the Ong, Soriano, Preciado-Cruz, and Olson Hong families, who have hosted our writing sessions, sponsored our trips, treated us to movie nights, and helped sustain us, especially through the pandemic. And thank you Lydia, Eunice, and Ayanna for your ongoing support.

Thank you to our community. Tú eres mi otro yo. You are my other me. Shout-out to Youth vs. Apocalypse (Carolyn Norr), Homies Empowerment (César Cruz, Jazmín Preciado), and blackyard arts (Ashley Herring). You are like second homes to us. Thank you to Af3IRM SF Bay Area, Urban Promise Academy community, 6th-grade team (Lisa Hiltbrand, Adrian Romero, Ann-Marie Gamble, Sam Clinton, Shannon Darcey, Nathaniel Ng), UPA Leadership (Tierre Mesa, Joseph Blasher, Claire Fisher, Dennis Guikema), UPA Gender Sexuality Alliance - Rainbow Club (Crystal Barajas Barr), UPA Girls Outdoor Club (Laura Young and

Kate Scott aka Ms. Krumrei), UPA Music Club (Gretchen Baglyos), UPA OEA organizing team (Laura, Adrian, David Conner, and Monica Yupa), UPA Family Resource Center (Glendy Cordero, Guadalupe Gomez Munguia), Jessica Alvarado, Dr. David Ramirez, Mary Ellen Bayardo, EBAYC Expanded Learning after school program (Freddy Mesa, Diego Rivera-García), Earth Guardians Bay Area Crew, BoomShake Music, Agency by Design Oakland, Oakland in the Middle, Anti Police-Terror Project, Abundant Beginnings, Sogorea Te' Land Trust, OUSD Ethnic Studies Cohort, OUSD Restorative Justice, OUSD Asian Pacific Islander Student Achievement (APISA) Initiative, People's Education Movement, Harvard Graduate School of Education (Steve Seidel and Kamila H. Muhammad), the Harvard Graduate School of Education Alumni of Color Conference (Christina Villareal), and Wah Lum Kung Fu and Tai Chi Academy in Malden (Andrea So and Sifu Mai Du).

Thank you to SF Jazz - Jazz in the Middle artists, including Tammy Hall and Dan Wolf - for encouraging us to share our story,

Thank you to Darius Simpson and Guisela Ramos for your support with poetry and writing workshops.

Thank you to Agustín Barajas Amaral and Crystal Barajas Barr (along with Adrianna Álvarez, Val Lizarraga, Inés & Vick) for your contribution to our work as visual artists.

Thank you to Oscar Cervantes, the Cervantes family, Los Hermanos staff, Rafael Perez, S&F Towing, Homies Empowerment, and volunteers (including Shira Bannerman, Maria Lourdes Nocedal-Geaga, and Nhi Truong) for your support with the community garden project at UPA.

Thank you jOn jOn and The Grease Diner for your help with screen printing, so that we have t-shirts and flags to represent our organization.

Thank you to the team at Nomadic Press, J. K. Fowler, Laura Salazar, Jevohn Tyler Newsome, and Michaela Mullin. Without your support, this dream of a project would not be a reality.

Thank you to our funders, Oakland Public Education Fund (A to Z Grant), Oakland Promise (Youth Organizer Grant), Agency by Design Oakland (individual community donors and Susan Wolf), and 49ers Foundation's Dr. Harry Edwards "Follow Your Bliss" Award grant, for valuing our work in material ways through your fiscal support.

Thank you to everyone who has supported our organizing work

over the years.

Thank you to the movement. Pick it up, pass it on, and keep it going! Finally, thank you to all of the journalists, writers, and photographers who conducted interviews and featured our work in previous publications or online. You have made us feel seen and heard over the years:

Anderson, Brooke. "Meet the Bay Area teens behind the Climate Strikes," *Medium.com*, October 1, 2019, https://medium.com/@brookeanderson/meet-the-bay-area-teens-behind-the-climate-strikes-6d49d78ef179

Bunker, Survival Media Agency, https://flic.kr/p/29NhmzL

First-Arai, Leanna. "It's Zombies Versus Coal in East Oakland: For Angelika Soriano, a prospective coal terminal sounded horrifying," *Sierra Club Magazine*, September 10, 2019, https://www.sierraclub.org/sierra/2019-5-september-october/act/its-zombies-versus-coal-east-oakland

Juhasz, Antonia. "A 12-Year-Old Warrior for Justice," *Ms. Magazine*, November 13, 2017, https://msmagazine.com/2017/11/13/12-year-old-warrior-justice/

Schatz, Kate. "Y is for Youth Climate Movement," *Rad American Movements A-Z: Movements and Moments That Demonstrate the Power of the People*, 151-155. Potter/Ten Speed/Harmony/Rodale, 2020.

Sunrise Movement, "These 10 Op-Eds from Youth Climate Strikers Explain Their Need to Take Action," *Medium.com*, March 18, 2019, https://medium.com/sunrisemvmt/these-10-op-eds-from-youth-climate-strikers-explain-their-need-to-take-action-c2891e983a6f

Vega, Anesti. Survival Media Agency, https://flic.kr/p/2aPnozS
Ibid. https://art.350.org/rise-murals/

# Aidyn May Robles

Aidyn May Robles (they/them) is a 14-year-old sophomore at Envision Academy. They are half-Mexican, half-Cambodian. In 6th grade, they attended a field trip where they were educated about the horrible effects climate change has on our environment. There, they learned about the Environmental Protection Agency holding a hearing in San Francisco, and that they were able to voice our opinions to them. That day, they spoke at both San Francisco City Hall and directly to the EPA about the effects climate change would have on our community and why they care. A few weeks later, Aidyn joined Warriors for Justice, to continue their fight for Climate Justice.

# Angelica Perkins

Angelica Perkins (she/her) was born and raised in Oakland, California, and went to O.U.S.D. schools her entire life. She is 19 years old and just began her sophomore year at San Francisco State University. She became a member of Warriors for Justice during its early days (2015) as a 7th-grader with a new passion for civil rights. Angelica was involved with the organization for the rest of middle school and much of high school.

# Angelika Soriano

Angelika Soriano (she/her) is a 16-year-old junior at Oakland High School. She became a member of Warriors for Justice when she was a 6th-grader at Urban Promise Academy and has been a member for six years. Along with Warriors for Justice, she's also a member and organizer of a Bay Area youth climate justice organization, Youth vs. Apocalypse. Through Warriors for Justice, Angelika has grown to use her voice and express her thoughts on the climate crisis through art, believing that our earth is on fire, and youth deserves a future.

# Christopher Soriano

Christopher Soriano (he/him) is 14 years old and a freshman at Oakland High school. He's been a member of Warriors for Justice since 6th grade. Through W4J, he's grown to become an environmental and climate justice youth activist fighting for his life and future generations. In addition to his work with W4J, Christopher is an organizer and member of the Bay Area youth climate justice organization, Youth vs. Apocalypse.

# Cory Jong

Cory Jong (she/they) supports youth-led organizing as an adult co-conspirator with Warriors for Justice and Youth vs. Apocalypse. Cory became a social justice educator based on their background in anti-imperialist organizing and a passion to create systemic change by arousing, organizing, and mobilizing the masses. As a person of Chinese ancestry born in Oakland (Huichin, occupied Ohlone territory), Cory teaches in the Fruitvale district of East Oakland. They are proud to be planting seeds for future generations, driven by the idea that "each generation, out of relative obscurity, must define its mission, fulfill it, or betray it," a message shared by Yuri Kochiyama, based on Frantz Fanon's work.

# Iyyah Zareef-Mustafa

Iyyah Zareef-Mustafa (she/her) supports and co-founded Warriors for Justice with Mx. Cory in 2016, when she was in 6th grade. Iyyah is a 17-year-old senior at MetWest Highschool. Iyyah began investing her time in activism, self education, and environmental change, in order to make positive change on social issues in communities. Throughout Warriors for Justice, she attended her first marches, poetry competition, and it was the first time she helped lead, plan, and organize in a school club. She has learned so much from Warriors for Justice, such as communication, teamwork, creativity, and more. Iyyah is very proud of and excited about what Warriors for Justice has in store for the future.

# Kai Hong

Kai Hong (he/him) is 13 years old and in 8th grade at Urban Promise Academy. He joined the Warriors for Justice in 6th grade, because he wanted to help make the world more like a family. Kai wants to show people who think they can do whatever they want to others, and to our planet, that what they are doing is not okay.

# Mariah Lazalde

Mariah Lazalde (she/her/they/them) is 17 years old and a senior at Metwest High School, in Oakland, CA. They became a member of W4J in 6th grade at Urban Promise Academy, after finding a passion for activism and Social Justice. They've been involved since the early days of W4J, and have been involved all throughout middle school and partially throughout high school. W4J has helped them grow their knowledge of what is going on in the world, and helped Mariah use their voice to create social change.

# Sonia Mendoza

Sonia Mendoza (she/her) is 16 years old and a Junior at MetWest High School Huggins Campus. She is a Warriors for Justice alumni, having joined in 6th grade, and is glad she did, because it went in depth with all the issues of the world. W4J is an important part of her growing up and being a youth activist, and that is when she became more aware of what was happening with the world. It has taught Sonia that as youth, they can do anything, and she's maintained that mentality.

# Santiago Preciado-Cruz

Santiago Preciado-Cruz (he/him) is 14 years old and a freshman at Life Academy. He is a proud Mexicano and an active member of Warriors for Justice. He was taught all his life that fighting for what is right is important, and when he got to UPA in 6th grade, was told about a social justice group, Warriors for Justice. He went to the Oratorical and saw people from his school participating, and wanted to do something too. Since then, Santiago has been an active member, and has been trying to educate himself and those around him about social justice.

# Sophia Lopez Garcia

Sophia Lopez Garcia (she/they) is a 15-year-old Chicana and a sopho-
more at Envision Academy. She is an alumni of Warriors for Justice, as of
last year. The reason she joined Warriors for Justice in 6th grade at UPA is
because she was already interested in helping her community; going to
the protest in front of the house of Phil Tagami (re: No Coal in Oakland)
was the step Sophia wanted in order to help her community.

# Tanaya Patton

Tanaya Patton (she/her) is 15 years old and in 11<sup>th</sup> grade. She is an alumnus of Warriors for Justice. When she was in the 6<sup>th</sup> grade, she joined W4J, which got her very interested in politics. She became involved in my community and campaigns, such as No Coal in Oakland. Her teacher, Ms. Lisa, directed her to W4J because of her interest in history and because Tanaya raised her hand a lot. She loves Harry Potter (she is a Ravenclaw) and also has an interest in golf.

# COVER MISSIVE

## On "Le Bien"

By Isaac Vazquez Avila
Instagram: @aliencitizen
Website: www.avilarosesigns.com

The way I approach the process of painting is guided in part by preliminary drawings of words, letters, patterns, shapes and objects from the real world that I recall from memory or analyze through photographs I take. I choose what subjects to paint when an image lingers in my head like friends who hangout on the corner block listening to music, sharing smoke and recalling stories of the past week on Friday night. Painting for me is an inexact process, guided by both reference and control and intuition and impulsivity. It is from here that my work and specifically "Le Bien" are generated from.

# OTHER WAYS TO SUPPORT NOMADIC PRESS' WRITERS

In 2020, two funds geared specifically toward supporting our writers were created: the **Nomadic Press Black Writers Fund** and the **Nomadic Press Emergency Fund**.

The former is a forever fund that puts money directly into the pockets of our Black writers. The latter provides dignity-centered emergency grants to any of our writers in need.

Please consider supporting these funds. You can also more generally support Nomadic Press by donating to our general fund via nomadicpress.org/donate and by continuing to buy our books. As always, thank you for your support!

Scan below for more information and/or to donate.
You can also donate at nomadicpress.org/store.